FORGOTTEN
TANKS AND GUNS

FORGOTTEN TANKS AND GUNS
OF THE 1920s, 1930s AND 1940s

DAVID LISTER

Pen & Sword
MILITARY

AN IMPRINT OF PEN & SWORD BOOKS LTD.
YORKSHIRE – PHILADELPHIA

First published in Great Britain in 2018.
This edition printed in 2021 by
Pen & Sword Military
An imprint of
Pen & Sword Books Ltd
Yorkshire – Philadelphia

Copyright © David Lister, 2018, 2021

ISBN 978 1 39901 432 8

The right of David Lister to be identified as Author of this work has been asserted by him in accordance with the Copyright, Designs and Patents Act 1988.

A CIP catalogue entry for this book is available from the British Library. All rights reserved. No part of this book may be reproduced or transmitted in any form or by any means, electronic or mechanical including photocopying, recording or by any information storage and retrieval system, without permission from the Publisher in writing.

Typeset in Times New Roman 11/13.5 by
SJmagic DESIGN SERVICES, India.

Printed and bound in the UK by CPI Group (UK) Ltd, Croydon, CR0 4YY

Pen & Sword Books Ltd includes the Imprints of Pen & Sword Aviation, Pen & Sword Family History, Pen & Sword Maritime, Pen & Sword Military, Wharncliffe Local History, Pen & Sword Select, Pen & Sword Military Classics, Leo Cooper, The Praetorian Press, Remember When, Seaforth Publishing and Frontline Publishing.

For a complete list of Pen & Sword titles please contact
PEN & SWORD BOOKS LIMITED
47 Church Street, Barnsley, South Yorkshire, S70 2AS, England
E-mail: enquiries@pen-and-sword.co.uk
Website: www.pen-and-sword.co.uk

Or
PEN AND SWORD BOOKS
1950 Lawrence Rd, Havertown, PA 19083, USA
E-mail: Uspen-and-sword@casematepublishers.com
Website: www.penandswordbooks.com

Contents

Foreword vii
Introduction for 2nd edition ix
Acknowledgements xi
Chapter 1   Lurking in the Jungle 1
Chapter 2   Battle Wing 15
Chapter 3   From the Sea, through the Blood to
                    the Green fields Beyond 21
Chapter 4   You Disston my Tank? 31
Chapter 5   The Smoking Gun 41
Chapter 6   Hail Hydran! 49
Chapter 7   The Cambridge Camal 53
Chapter 8   Schwimmpanzer 36 59
Chapter 9   Recoil Control 63
Chapter 10   The Soldierless Tank 67
Chapter 11   The Secret Life of the Infantry Tank 77
Chapter 12   The Tanks without a War 97
Postscript 127
Sources 129

Foreword

Since 2013 I have been delving into archives as part of my consultancy work on military history. This has led to my viewing files that have not been viewed by historians before whether they had been misfiled, or just not been specific enough for other historians to request. There have been many odd finds: some if not all have not been enough for more than a few paragraphs about them and the file's contents.

A few years ago one of my friends pointed out I had a lot of projects that history had forgotten and suggested that I compile them into a book. This idea launched the project that has finally resulted in this book. It has taken some time to compile all the plans, drawings and files, as well as writing the actual document but I hope you will enjoy it.

So please let me show you a collection of invention, genius and optimistic thought that results in a selection of history's lost tanks and guns.

David Lister

For more history, including weekly articles:

www.historylisty.com
www.facebook.com/historylisty

Introduction for 2nd edition

In the three years since this book was first published it has generated some discussion, nearly all of it concentrated around the Japanese tanks. Like all books, they are only a discussion of what is known at that time, and inevitably more information will come to light. Due to only having limited space, and not being able to modify the text for the 2nd edition, this addendum is now an errata of the chapters, concentrating on the Japanese tank section.

Some of the comments about the Japanese tanks were entirely negative, including the accusations that I had manufactured the designs and falsified the supporting paperwork. In part, this is my fault for providing a shockingly bad sources list.

This claim is entirely false. The sources for the tanks in the chapter, and their supporting plans can be found at the UK National Archives at Kew, under the following file references:

- WO 208/1320 Armoured fighting vehicles; characteristics and performance with photographs and drawings.
- WO 208/1325 Armoured fighting vehicles; heavy tanks.

It should be noted that several files around the same document reference cover other aspects of Japanese armour such as WO 208/1324 which covers light tanks, or 1327 which is concerned with amphibious designs. However, these other files just contain information on known tank designs.

It seems that the same plans used in the Ishi-108 (page 9) were found in a British document talking about the A1E1 Independent, although it was not a wholly accurate drawing, which led me to consider the Ishi-108 a slightly modified copy of the A1E1. This idea that the Japanese engineers were copying other plans does lead us nicely to the next point. In most cases, the Japanese claimed performance seems a tad optimistic when you look at it, especially around the engine, their output and the tanks speeds. From those facts, we can form the suggestion that the designs of the tanks are proposed plans and estimated performance.

That being said I still consider it a strong possibility that the Type 97 heavy tank (page 3 and 4) did get somewhere as a project as we have other sources for it, albeit we still lack the undeniable proof of a photograph.

A suspicion I have for the presence of the heavy tank designs is that the Japanese asked the three companies to submit plans for the next design of heavy tank, and the Ishi-108, AI-96 (Page 5), and Type 97 were submitted. Of course, this is a hypothesis on my behalf and fails to explain items like the Mitsu-104 (page 6) which came from the same company as the Type 97, or the differing designations, which usually relate to years.

In good news, the Kawasaki 2594 (page 11) has been discovered, or at least something that hints at a strong familial link. There is a Japanese amphibious tank wreck at the Kokopo War Museum in Papua New Guinea, Which bears a striking resemblance to the 2594, at least the hull does. Of course, nothing is straightforward, and the superstructure is different to the plans.

The differences in the superstructure once again hint that the plan in the files is a proposed design. Often during tank development things like this will change due to modifications forced upon the designers by things like weight considerations. At least two photographs of the tank undergoing testing have been discovered as well.

Finally, the tank in the photograph on page 3 has been positively identified, and it is not the Ishi 2598, but instead is likely to be the Type 98 Ke-Ni light tank. Although it should be pointed out that again there are strong resemblances in the hull and suspension, as well as both being dated the same year. In this case, however, the producing companies appear to be different.

Acknowledgements

Seon Eun Ae: for her help with the Japanese tanks.
www.sensha-manual.blogspot.co.uk

Ed Francis: proof-reading and sharing information.

Paul Charlton: editing

Andrew Hills: for being a tank-obsessed friend I could discuss my findings with, digging through patents and for sharing information.

Teodor S. Angheluta and Andrei Kirushkin: for their artwork.

The Members of 'The Shop' channel: for random help and assistance during the writing of this book.

Note on plans
The plans in 'Lurking in the Jungle' are more basic than ones later in the book and are designed to show the basic arrangements of the tanks. This is in part due to the condition of the original documents which were printed on a much glossier paper than we might find normal today. As a result, much of the image has been degraded over time. Equally, to keep the plans simple, many of the fixtures and the details have been omitted.

Chapter 1

Lurking in the Jungle

The work of an intelligence officer is not easy because of a mixture of enemy disinformation, the varying quality of material supplied to you and your own preconceived notions and prejudices. Take, for example, the subject of Japanese heavy tanks. The common perception today is that the Japanese heavy tank projects never progressed past a handful of experimental designs and one rather hopeful super-heavy project during the Second World War. Beyond that, it is commonly thought that the Japanese did not field any heavy tanks.

During the Second World War nearly every nation had some form of heavy tank, and it was known to the British, from reliable sources, that the Japanese had been experimenting on the class. It was expected that the Japanese would at some point start to use them, and British intelligence tried to keep a track on Japanese tank development.

Among the sources that fed information back to the UK was the British military attaché in Tokyo. One such report was about a Japanese tank exhibition between 10 and 16 February 1939. Held at the Yasukuni Shrine,

A line of tanks at a Japanese display, perhaps even the one at Yasukuni Shrine. The tank nearest the camera is a Type 94 tankette; next is a Type 92 heavy armoured car. The rearmost tank is a Type 89 of some variant, but in between it and the Type 92 is an unidentified tank. From the limited view of this picture it seems to match the Ishi 2598 (see Page 13).

the purpose was to allow the public to view tanks and armoured vehicles, some captured in China, others domestically built. The collection was drawn up in two rows on either side of the shrine and enclosed by barriers allowing people to get no closer than about six feet. Photography was banned and the area swamped with *Kempeitai* officers to make sure this was obeyed. The military attaché, Major T.G. Wards, however, visited the exhibition and filed a report on what he saw. Major Wards noted that, as a foreign observer, his actions were closely monitored and he was unable to give each tank more than a passing glance due to the presence of the *Kempeitai*.

The first exhibit was captured material, such as Chinese armoured cars, which were civilian trucks which had been armoured. Something referred to as an 'Ansard' light tank, which weighed three tons and had a crew of two and two machine guns, was possibly an Ansaldo CV.3, an Italian tankette.

Next came the Japanese tanks, starting with a heavy tank. The heavy tank Wards saw may have been the Experimental II with a main gun in both the turret and the hull, and a mini-turret at the rear housing a machine gun. One of the other exhibits was a Type 89 I-Go that had seen action in China. It had been taken under heavy small-arms fire and was claimed to have been hit about a thousand times.

After the war started sources became harder to come by. Intelligence officers had to make do with incomplete snippets of information, or information from prisoner of war interrogations. Some such interrogations seem to have muddied the waters, e.g. from these it appears that the Type 97 Chi-Ha was often mistaken for a heavy tank.

One prisoner of war was a lieutenant in the 1st Independent Mixed Regiment on Saipan, captured in July 1944. He stated that the Type 97 Chi-Ha had 15mm of armour and a twelve-cylinder diesel engine; his unit had trained on them in August 1941. He also claimed that all tanks had radios, air conditioning and twin 47mm guns, with one mounted in the standard turret and another in the hull and that they could fit thirty ammunition boxes in the tank, each box being 2-feet long, 1-foot tall and 1.5-feet wide. Finally, and most bizarrely, he claimed that, as well as one drive wheel at the front, it had two smaller drive wheels at the back, both 14 inches across. The intelligence report indicated that this might signify an earlier model suspension. The prisoner of war also gave a rundown of crew numbers: three men for this particular medium tank, two for a light tank and an unknown number for a heavy tank.

Another report was from a private who had been captured on Manus Island. Wounded, he sought help from natives who, unsurprisingly, promised to help but simply turned him over to the US forces sometime around 6 August 1944.

An example of a sketch drawn by a prisoner of war. This particular one accompanied the intelligence report about the Type 97 heavy tank.

In civilian life he had been a foreman at the Hitachi forging plant at Kameari where he had been working up until at least November 1943. Whilst there, he had seen several of Japan's heavy tank, the Type 97, and claimed that the Type 97 heavy was 22-feet long, 8.5-feet tall and 9-feet wide, weighing in at twenty-seven tons. Protected by 30mm of armour, its 300hp engine could move it at 15mph while it could climb a 35-degree slope and had a crew of six.

The Japanese did have plans for a Type 97 heavy tank but it was built by Mitsubishi, and was known as the Mitsu-97. The numbers given by the prisoner of war were very close to those for the tank. The British had obtained several plans of Japanese tanks, including the Mitsu-97 and the plans appear to be genuine. Even the type, finish and size of the paper matches that used by the Japanese, which is different from that used by the British at that time.

Type 97 Heavy Tank
(Mitsu-97 heavy tank)

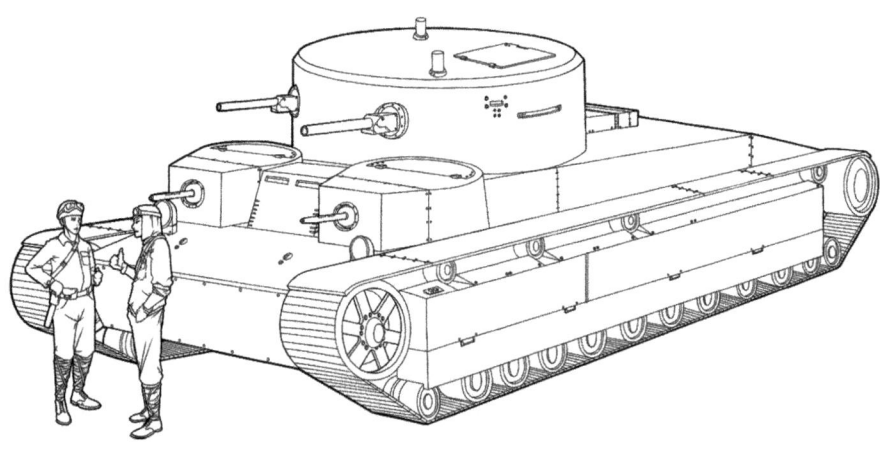

Manufacturer	Mitsubishi	Engine	Water-cooled Mitsubishi 12-cylinder giving 250hp
Length	7.45m	Slope	45 degrees
Width	3m	Vertical obstacle	1m
Height	2.93m	Trench crossing	2.11m
Weight	32 tonnes	Speed	28mph
Armour	22-35mm	Weapons	Two cannon and four machine guns
Crew	Six	Ammunition	350 shells

LURKING IN THE JUNGLE

Ai-96
(Heavy tank)

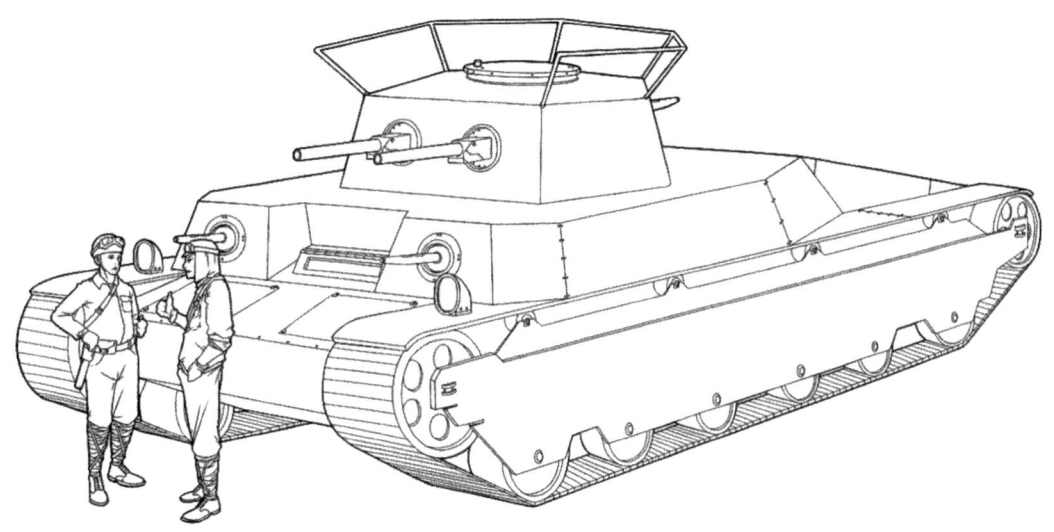

Manufacturer	Aichi	Engine	Air- and water-cooled Aichi V12 giving 350hp
Length	9.35m	Slope	40 degrees
Width	3.25m	Vertical obstacle	0.76m
Height	2.75m	Trench crossing	1.25m
Weight	36 tonnes	Speed	36mph
Armour	25-35mm	Weapons	Twin 37mm or a single 75mm. Three machine guns
Crew	10	Ammunition	500 shells

Mitsu-104
(Heavy tank)

Manufacturer	Mitsubishi	Engine	Water-cooled Mitsubishi 12-cylinder giving 250hp
Length	8.3m	Slope	45 degrees
Width	3.2m	Vertical obstacle	1.2m
Height	2.8m	Trench crossing	3.9mm
Weight	29 tonnes	Speed	25mph
Armour	25-30mm	Weapons	One 75mm, and two machine guns. Two machine guns, or two 37mm guns, in sub-turrets.
Crew	Eight	Ammunition	250 shells

LURKING IN THE JUNGLE

A Japanese postcard showing what is seems to be an Ai-96. Above it a Type 97 Chi-Ha for comparison. From this you can see that the silhouette and scale of the tank is very different.

The details of these tanks were all found in files stored in the UK, although some of the details were written in French. This might be because the documents were translated from Japanese to French first, due to French being the language of diplomacy. Several of the tanks had dates for their entry into service: the Mitsu-97, for example, had an in-service date of 9 November 1936, and the Ai-96's date was 1 February 1937. If this is true, and the prisoner of war report suggests it might be, then these are two Japanese heavy tanks that have been forgotten about since the Second World War. Part of the problem is that even sources like the US Intelligence briefings, which seem to be drawn from UK sources, have mentioned Type 97 heavy tanks previously but for the last seventy years every historian, myself included, who has glanced at these documents discounted the information as mis-identifications. It is not helped by the Type 97 heavy tank sharing the same number as the Type 97 Chi-Ha medium tank.

As well as the prisoner of war eyewitness reports, there is other supporting evidence, including a late-1930s postcard that shows, in silhouette, what could be an Ai-96. Tantalisingly, as it is just the shape of the tank with a few tiny details, it is hard to get a full identification but the size of the crew indicated in the image does give credence to the idea that the tank was rather large. As well as the size of the tank, if it was a Type 97 Chi-Ha, then the turret would have been offset to one side rather than covering the full width of the hull.

Two other heavy tanks are mentioned in the UK sources. One, in 1934, was the 'Showa 10' but, apart from listing its armaments as two cannon and several machine guns, no further detail was given. It does say that several 'Showa 10' had been landed in China which was also where documents suggest the Mitsu-104 served. This is reinforced by a document found in the Japanese national archives in which a logistics officer in China requested more supplies of '7cm tank gun ammunition'. In the pre-war period the only Japanese tanks with 7cm guns were their heavy tanks. All the previously known models of heavy tanks, such as the Experimental II, did not leave the Japanese home islands which leaves the Mitsu-104 or 'Showa 10' as possibly the best candidates for such ammunition requests.

The final heavy tank was reported to the British in July 1941. It was called the Ishi-108 and, in appearance, resembled a British Vickers A.1E1 Independent. There were some physical differences between the two. The Ishi-108 was bigger, being over two metres longer and a metre wider; however it was not as high as the Independent. The Ishi-108 also weighed in at about eight tons more while the armour is stated to be 8mm less. The main change was the weaponry. Whereas the A.1E1 had a single 3-pounder 47mm gun in the turret and several machine guns in mini-turrets, the Ishi-108 had two hull turrets carrying 37mm guns and a third with a flamethrower. The main turret was armed with a 7cm tank gun. This did appear to cause some confusion in the translations, as the direct translation has three 'turret' guns listed. The British originally seem to have thought that all this wide selection of weapons was arrayed in the main turret.

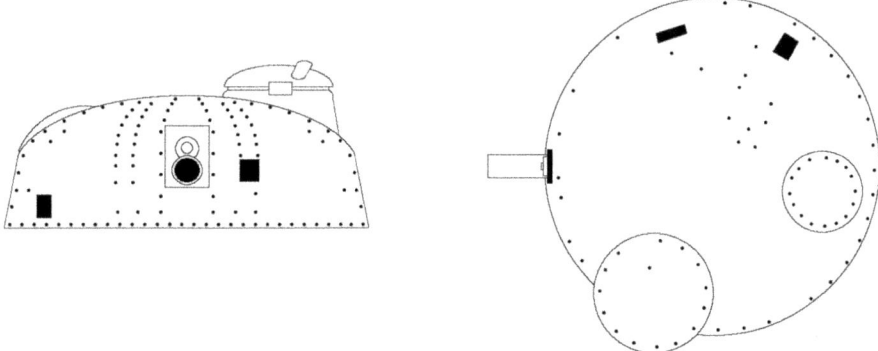

The turret of the Ishi-108. At first glance it looks very much like the A1E1 Independent turret. However, the position of the commander's cupola has been moved from the rear to the left side, and another structure added to the opposite side of the turret, where there is normally a ventilator.

\multicolumn{4}{c}{Ishi-108}			
Manufacturer	Ishikawajima	Engine	water cooled 12 cylinder giving 350hp
Length	9.75m	Turret Weapons	Two 37mm's or one 75mm
Width	3.5m		
Height	2.8m		
Weight	38 tonnes	Ammunition	750 shells for the 75mm
Armour	20-30mm	Hull weapons	Three machine guns, one flamethrower
Crew	Twelve	Speed	30mph

Translation difficulties also account for a possible mistake in the armour thickness. Most of the armour thicknesses listed for these tanks seem to be quite thin, at just 35mm. This could be down to the way the Japanese constructed their heavy tanks, using a frame of structural armour of 35mm. Onto this they seem to have bolted on additional armour plate to reach the desired thickness. Therefore it is possible that the armour values recorded on the documents simply refer to the structural armour. This theory is backed up by later heavy tanks such as the O-I, which some plans show having 35mm structural plate. In addition, a Soviet intelligence report detailing other nations' tanks mentions the Type 97 heavy tank as having 65mm of armour.

The quality of Japanese armour plate also came under scrutiny by the British. Samples of 6mm, 9mm and 12mm plate were taken from a Japanese light tank and subjected to tests and it was found to be homogenous plate. The testing also included firing at the plate samples with everything from .303 rifles, .55 Boys anti-tank rifles and larger calibre anti-tank guns. The 6mm plate was the equivalent of good quality British plate while the 9mm was even better quality. However, the thicker 12mm plate performed terribly which was judged to be down to the depth of face hardening, which only amounted to about 9-10 per cent of the depth of the plate.

The final note on heavy tanks recorded by the British came from a report in August 1944. It warned that the Japanese had developed a 54-ton tank armed with a 4-inch gun and a flamethrower, although no further details were forthcoming. The Japanese were developing a 105mm high-velocity tank gun in that period, a weapon originally destined for a self-propelled tank destroyer.

Development of these projects was halted by the end of the Second World War. On 5 September Major General Iguchi, commander of 80th Division, signed a surrender document for the Japanese army in the Philippines. It is his official seal that is on most of the tank plans recovered by the British.

As well as the heavy tanks above, the files also included original Japanese designs for light tanks.

LURKING IN THE JUNGLE

(Kawasaki) Kawa 2594
(Amphibious tank)

Manufacturer	Kawasaki	Engine	Air-cooled Kawasaki 6-cylinder giving 220hp
Length	4.5m	Slope	42 degrees
Width	2.4m	Vertical obstacle	0.5m
Height	2.7m	Trench crossing	1.1m
Weight	4 tonnes	Speed	25mph/6 knots
Armour	15-20mm	Weapons	37mm or machine gun in turret.
Crew	Two	Ammunition	120 shells

FORGOTTEN TANKS AND GUNS OF THE 1920s, 1930s AND 1940s

Mitsubishi 2592 (1932)
(Light tank)

Manufacturer	Mitsubishi	Engine	Mitsubishi 12-cylinder water-cooled giving 280hp
Length	4.75m	Slope	35 degrees
Width	2.1m	Vertical obstacle	0.65m
Height	2m	Weapons	37mm or 75mm gun, one machine gun in turret. One machine gun in hull
Weight	4.5 tonnes		
Armour	9-25mm	Speed	22mph (a larger engine could take it up to 37mph)
Crew	five	Ammunition	200 shells

LURKING IN THE JUNGLE

2599 (1939) Mitsubishi
(Light tank)

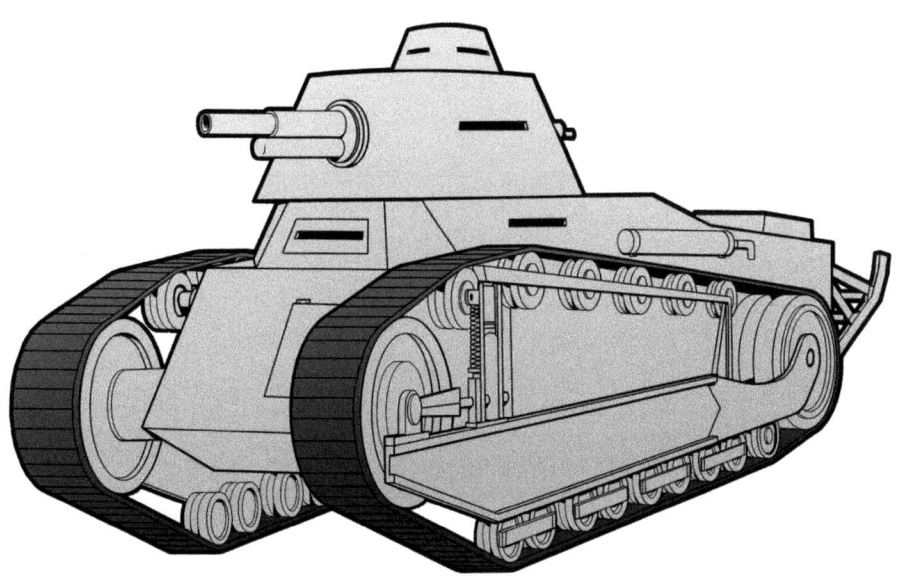

Manufacturer	Mitsubishi	Engine	Mitsubishi 6-cylinder water-cooled giving 45hp
Length	5.34m	Slope	40 degrees
Width	2.54m	Vertical obstacle	0.65m
Height	2.65m	Trench crossing	2.55m
Weight	12 tonnes	Speed	24mph
Armour	6-17mm	Weapons	one 37mm and machine gun in the turret.
Crew	three	Ammunition	250 shells

FORGOTTEN TANKS AND GUNS OF THE 1920s, 1930s AND 1940s

Ishi 2598

Manufacturer	Ishikawajima	Engine	Ishikawajima air- and water-cooled 4-cylinder giving 55hp
Length	3.15m	Slope	34 degrees
Width	1.76m	Vertical obstacle	0.65m
Height	1.63m	Trench crossing	0.85m
Weight	3 tonnes	Speed	-
Armour	8-14mm	Weapons	one 37mm gun, one hull machine gun
Crew	3	Ammunition	-

Chapter 2

Battle Wing

Early in the Second World War the British started working on their ideas for airborne troops. Among the subjects considered was an airborne tank, and how to deliver it to the battlefield. With the fledgling airborne force in place and beginning to expand, the British turned their attention to the idea, and more importantly how to fly the tank to the drop zone. Their first thoughts were a conventional glider design, which would, eventually, become the Hamilcar.

In late 1942 a novel and new idea was supplied from the Patent Office, although the patent had first been applied for in 1941. It came from Alan Muntz and Company, based at Heston Airport who called it the 'Carden-Baynes Air

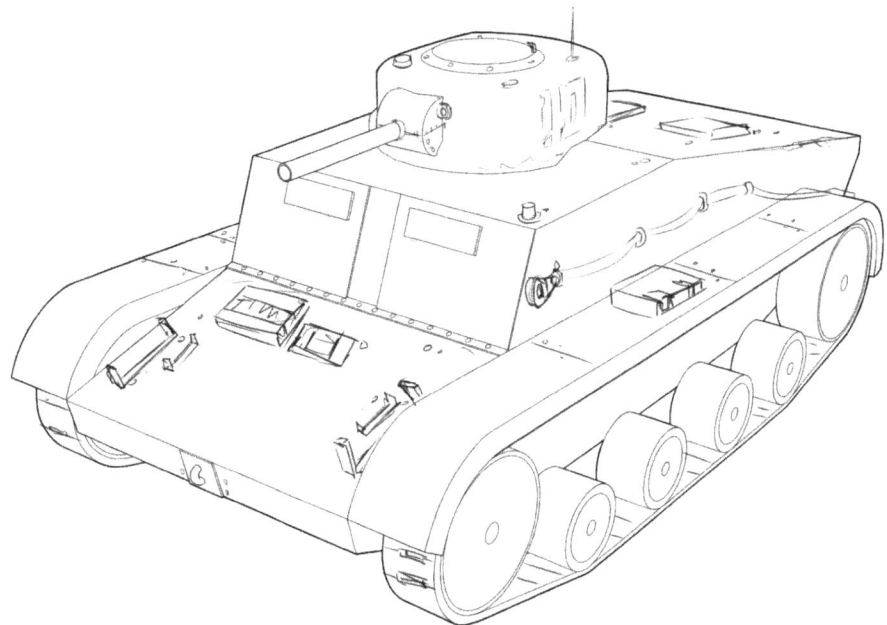

Artist's impression of the Carden-Baynes light tank, based upon the plans submitted to the War Office.

Tank'. The 'Baynes' part of the name probably came from L.E. Baynes of Slingsby Sailplanes Ltd, a manufacturer of gliders, based at Kirkbymoorside.

The design was a flying wing, with the tank slung in the middle, and the turret inside the wing cross-section so that only the tracks and lower hull protruded under the wing. The tank's driver would also double as the pilot. Just before touchdown, the tracks were brought up to maximum speed and then, as the tank touched down, the suspension compressed. This was linked to an automatic release which disengaged the locks holding the wing to the hull of the tank. The combined mass was still travelling at near touchdown speeds, which meant that the wing was still generating a significant amount of lift but, since it was several tons lighter, it was lifted upwards and flipped away.

This left the tank travelling at full speed and battle-ready; all the crew had to do was to rotate the turret from its carry position, which was pointing to the aft of the tank. Mr Muntz seemed to have (although he never directly pushed this idea) the mental picture of these things landing directly into battle.

Muntz also went on to point out that his design had significant savings in manufacturing and material costs. As well as that, his proposal was quicker into action compared to unloading a conventional glider, with the added bonus that the pilot was better protected against enemy fire. The points about ease of manufacture and cost savings caught the interest of Lord Beaverbrook, the minister for war production. Beaverbrook's attention meant that, despite the Carden-Baynes glider not meeting the requirements of the general staff, who had issued specifications for a tank-carrying glider, the concept was investigated further. Normally this lack of adherence to the

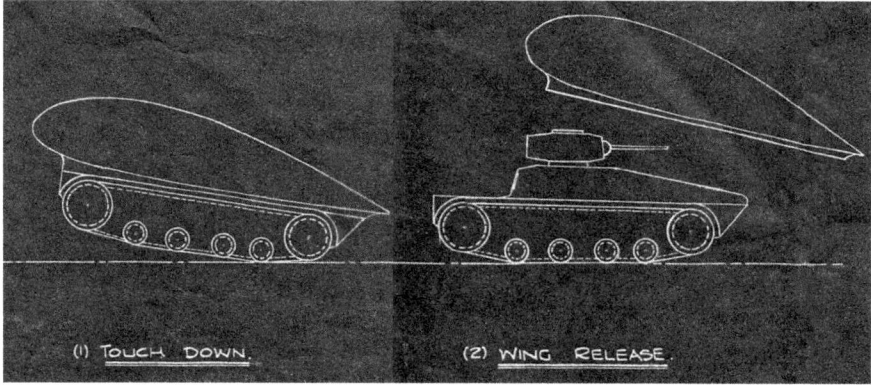

Original blue prints depicting how a Carden-Baynes light tank would touch down, and wing-release would occur. You can see the location of the turret rotated to the rear.

M22 Locust being unloaded from a Hamilcar glider.

requirements would have been a halted any project. However, the advantages were enough that Lord Beaverbrook kept the project moving.

One of the real concerns from the start of the project was the ability of the tracks to cope with the high speeds needed for landing and take off. Before that question could be answered, the British had to first decide which tank to use. Although the original proposal had contained a light tank designed by Muntz, it was easier to select an existing light tank than go through the entire development and testing process.

There were two main contenders, the T9 and the A.25, better known by their more common names, the M22 Locust and the Light Tank, Mk VIII, Harry Hopkins. The Harry Hopkins was selected simply because it was the only light tank in production, or about to come into production at the time, although some concerns were raised about its combat effectiveness. If the tracks could not take the speeds required, there was a back-up plan to use an armoured car. That way, upon landing, the car could have its clutch disengaged and just roll to a stop. The armoured cars considered were the Daimler, Coventry, AEC and a mystery armoured car referred to in documents as the 'Ford armoured car'. The last-named was about fourteen tons with a speed of 45mph, 50mm of armour, and armed with 57mm M1 gun.

The speed that the tracks had to run at was 65mph, which caused some concern with the engine manufacturers, Henry Meadows Ltd. That speed would require the engine to be run at 4,000rpm for short periods and,

The Baynes Bat in flight.

during touchdown, the suspension would also need to resist the forces from impact. Tests on the lighter Tetrarch had shown that the Meadows engine could be run at the required speeds for short periods with no negative effect. The Harry Hopkins' speed had previously been tested, easily doing 57mph, and on one occasion taking a 3-foot ramp in a jumping test at 40mph. The suspension had been designed to withstand impacts of six times the force of gravity. With all this in hand, the Harry Hopkins had passed the requirements.

Next the wing itself came under scrutiny. Prior to this the only work on tailless aircraft had been done in 1924 by Geoffrey Hill and Westland Aircraft Ltd. It seems that the work was forgotten about by the departments involved, and so they believed they were the first to attempt to design a tailless aircraft. Thus the project was received with some concern about how quickly the design could be introduced into service as, by then, the Allies were beginning to consider D Day, and needed this idea operational for an airborne assault. The perceived lack of research would mean developing the technology from scratch, but it was decided that some work should be carried out. Initially, scale models were built and a scale replica with a pilot's seat in a pod-like structure was constructed. The model appears to have been called the 'Baynes Bat', and first flew in July 1943. It turned out that the calculations for the wing loading had been wildly optimistic which left the designers with two options to make the scheme work: increase the required landing speed to 85-90mph, or substantially increase the size of the glider wing. While Vickers Ltd was confident about the Harry Hopkins doing

A Universal carrier, having been unloaded next to a Hamilcar glider during Operation VARSITY, the Rhine crossing, in March 1945.

65mph they baulked at the idea of 85mph. The larger wing size led to many problems, not least practicability of storage and taxiing. It also reduced the advantages the original scheme had in savings of material and costs.

The final problem was the general staff operational requirement which required the carriage of cargo and multiple lighter vehicles, such as a pair of Universal carriers or Jeeps. The Carden-Baynes wing could not carry either. An additional negative was that, if after the battle the wing was recovered and needed to be flown somewhere, a special attachment to simulate the weight of the tank and give the pilot somewhere to sit would be required. None of these problems applied to the conventional design.

With all this in mind the project was wound up. However, the information remained on the secret list until just after the Second World War ended when the Ministry of Supply, after being asked several times, formally released the Carden-Baynes wing from the list.

Chapter 3

From the Sea, through the Blood to the Green fields Beyond

From the Johnson Light infantry tank in the early 1920s through to the Duplex Drive tanks of the Second World War it would appear that there was no development work on amphibious tanks in the UK. Vickers did design a couple of two-man amphibious tanks in the 1930s, but these were not effective combat machines, being almost unarmoured and armed only with a machine gun. Yet the machine did find some overseas sales, most notably to Russia, who developed the tank into the T-37A. The British did develop some wooden floats that could be attached to a Vickers light tank to enable it to cross bodies of water but, apart from that, the common misconception is that Britain did not carry out any research or development into amphibious tanks.

During the first years of the Second World War Britain devoted some time and effort to designs and studies into operating tanks across water. By sheer coincidence, some private individuals were also thinking of this problem and came up with some ideas on the subject.

The first tank to receive a mention in the historical record was just such a private venture. On 2 July 1940 William Train Gray, of Altrincham, Chester, filed a patent for an amphibious tank but no plans or drawings were included with the application. Mr Gray's novel idea was termed a 'longitudinal' tank with a series of sections rotating around a single axis. One section held the tank's fighting compartment and crew, and remained the same way up at all times, while the others had tracks on the bottom and boat-like elements, such as propellers, hull and rudders on the top. When entering the water the front section would rotate through 180 degrees, leaving the tracks on the top and the boat on the bottom. The same would happen when the rear section entered the water. The process was reversed when leaving the water. For obvious reasons, the idea does not seem to have even been looked at by the government's scientific bodies.

The government itself was alive to the idea of amphibious tanks. Throughout 1940 there was some thought going into the concept of amphibious tanks, their design and operation. Although some experiments had been carried out on submersible tanks, including a cruiser Mk I being modified to drive along under water and managing to operate in water ten-feet deep. Initially thoughts were of infantry tanks being submersible for river crossings and the like, and cruiser tanks being supported by flotation devices. For landings from the sea, submersible designs were less favoured, and the development moved away from submersion. One idea put forward was the concept of building 'the battle landships of the Army'. These were seen more as boats with tracks and were in the 800-850-ton range. Lord William Douglas Weir, the man behind these ideas, pointed out that tracked machines of 1,200 tons already existed. With a warship's level of armour they would be able to ignore field artillery and would crush any known obstacle.

This idea was seen as too outlandish and the task of designing an amphibious tank and defining the requirements of the tank were handed to the Department of Naval Land Engineering (DNLE), which had previously designed the 'Nellie' trench-digging machine. The general staff requirement envisioned that the landings would consist of about 100 tanks in the first wave, launched from about 200 yards offshore. After landing, the tanks would need to fight and be able to secure a bridgehead about three to five miles in depth to cover follow-on waves. The War Office wanted the tanks in production by 1 April 1941. The short timescale meant that some of the more difficult propositions, such as submersion, were again dismissed which upset some parts of the development team as they had designed and were working on a submersible tank. The new DNLE tank was known simply as the AT-1, with the 'AT' standing for Amphibious tank. The design included track propulsion when in the water, which had some bearing on the next design we will study.

On 28 August 1940 an envelope with some plans and a covering letter landed on a desk in London in the Department for Scientific Research (DSR), and was then passed onto the DNLE for comment as they were working on amphibious tanks. The letter was from Matthew Cargin, of Wolley Avenue, New Farnley, Leeds, and in it he proposed a pair of new amphibious vehicles, both called the WLT. One stood for 'Water and Land Tank', the other 'Water and Land Transport'. These monsters were just over 49 feet in length and 17 feet in width, and weighed between 235 and 265 tons. The ground pressure for the 'WLT' tank was a surprisingly low 1.25kg/cm^2. In comparison, Germany's super-heavy Maus was 1.45kg/cm^2. Mr Cargin helpfully gave options for the tanks and transports. The Types 1 and 2 were both tanks with conical revolving turrets, the only difference between the two being the arrangement of their tracks. Type 1 had four tracks mounted on two independent turntables while Type 2 had its four

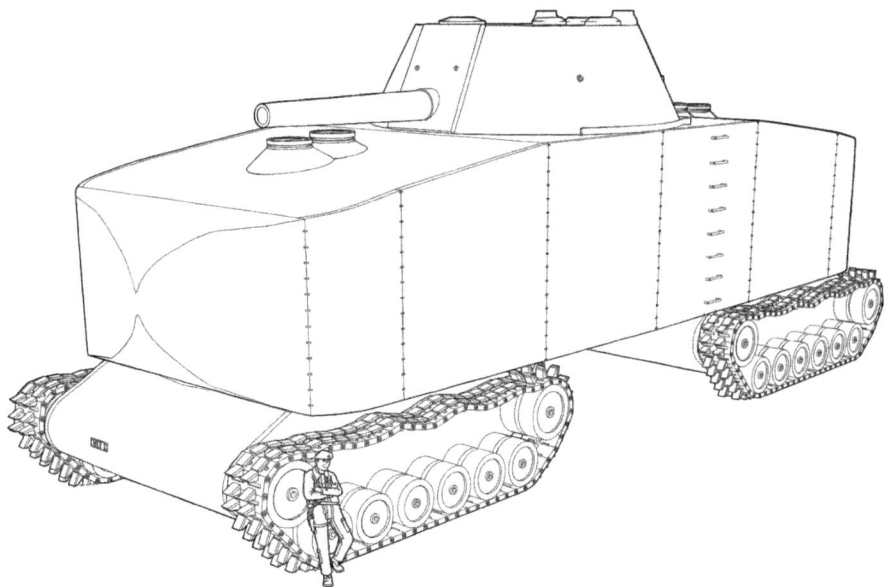

Artist's impression of the colossal WLT Type 1, drawn from the plans submitted by Mr Cargin. The unique pads on the tracks are extended on the leading edge of the tracks, and are changing their aspect on the top rear of the track unit that has the soldier standing next to it.

tracks mounted directly to the hull in a much more conventional method. Most had four engines in the 225bhp range, although the Transport Type 2 had twin 375bhp engines. Endurance was about eight days of continuous use with land speeds ranging from 38mph to 60mph. Maximum water speed for all was about 11 knots. The transports could carry eleven men as well as supplies to keep them fed and watered for the tank's full endurance.

One of Cargin's proposals was to increase either the armour thickness or firepower of the WLT tanks, although he did warn that increasing either meant that the vehicles would no longer be amphibious. Cargin did not list the armament but the WLT tank plans show what looks like a 9.2-inch gun, and the weapon's dimensions on the plan match those of the BL 9.2-inch gun Mk X.

The tracks themselves, for all four types, had pads that flipped out to help propel the vehicle through the water. The tracks would always turn in the same direction but a control could be set for forward or astern. When in 'forward gear', the pads on the bottom of the track would flip out, and the pads on the top part of the track run would close; for 'astern' the opposite was the case. This created paddles pushing in the desired direction. On land the pads on the tracks were all closed up. This particular feature was praised, along with the ingenuity of Mr Cargin in working out the idea. However, nearly every other element of his design, including ventilation and armour thickness, came in for some condemnation. The track design, while ingenious, was considered too complex for use and most of Cargin's calculations were also considered suspect. As a final point, the DNLE, who were working on track propulsion, were concerned about where Cargin had got the idea, and asked for MI5 to investigate him. At the time, due to the level of ingenuity Cargin had shown, the Department for Scientific Research was considering offering him a job. In a few short weeks over Christmas 1940 MI5 were able to put a complete dossier together on Mr Cargin:

> Age 42. Married. Born in Newcastle of Scottish parents. Ship engineer by trade. Was apprenticed at Newcastle-upon-Tyne and subsequently worked on the ships of many firms. In 1925 he went to Canada where he worked as a Draughtsman in various employments until he returned to this country in 1932. Believed since 1932 to have had one period of employment only, namely for some three months in 1939 as a Draughtsman with John Fowler (Leeds) Ltd. There was routine work at a wage averaging £3 10. 0. a week and he was not a very efficient workman. Absent sick on many occasions and eventually left of his own accord. Present source of income believed to be from property owned by his wife. No criminal records in Leeds district known and no observations arise under S.A.55.

This less than glowing reference caused him to be dropped from the DSR's recruitment list, and a letter of rejection for the WLT project was sent out.

Things went quiet for a period before, in late 1940, Mr Cargin reappeared. He had spent the intervening months drawing up detailed plans of the ventilators and other components to prove that his ideas were correct. He then started bombarding government departments with letters, sometimes at a rate of one a day. His letters went varyingly to the Ministry of Supply, the DSR and the Prime Minister's office and were mostly identical. At one point he sent in a letter demanding to know when his plan would be taken up by the British. Another he wrote to the DSR asked if they had received his letter, which he had sent to the Prime Minister's office only a couple of days before.

In his letters to the Prime Minister's office, Cargin answered the DNLE's complaint about the armour thickness of the tanks. He also laid out how these were war-winning weapons. On the armour thickness, he pointed out the armour plate was made of chromium-steel which, unfortunately, Cargin seemed to think would offer protection far in advance of normal armour. He may well have been right in the First World War but, by 1940, armour technology had moved on. Several times Mr Cargin took great pains to point out this perceived advantage in armour.

The second point he raised was how his WLTs would win the war, and the peace afterwards. First, just 500 WLT tanks and a similar number of WLT transports would be needed. This force would land directly into Germany from the mouth of the Rhine to the Kiel Canal. As follow-on forces held the coast and pushed slowly inland, the WLTs would charge along the Kiel Canal to the Baltic and down the Rhine. Then, with the flank secure, the force, again led by the WLTs, would push on into the heart of Berlin. Cargin also offered an alternative plan – landing in the area of Rotterdam to Dunkirk, then pushing on to the Baltic and Frankfurt and thence to Berlin. To defeat the Japanese, he forecast the same number of WLTs would be needed, although he failed to mention how they should be used.

Having won the war with just 1,000 tanks, Cargin turned his prowess towards the peace. The WLT transport, he predicted, would be able to handle heavy goods transport and so eliminate the need for expensive ports. A factory could just load its goods onto a waiting WLT which would then drive to the coast and sail to the nearest coast to the destination before driving the last leg overland. There followed a list of countries where the WLT transport would sell well as a guaranteed commercial success. This list included pretty much every land mass in the world apart from Russia and Europe. Mr Cargin closes his letter with the following line about his scheme: 'would require £20,000,000 capital for initial success.' That is nearly £1.2 billion today.

In the first quarter of 1941 Vickers had come up with a slightly more sensible idea for an amphibious tank, although it too used unusual armour. The Vickers submission was a much more conventional design, carrying three crewmen. The turret resembled a Tetrarch tank's turret and was similarly armed. It only weighed about 5.5 tons, to achieve which lightness it hardly had any equipment: even the radio was removed. Interestingly it had a built-in propeller shaft, driven by a power take-off from the engine. Armou- wise it was made from the highest quality aluminium, created by the use of electrolytic process, an expensive way to create armour. The armour was relatively thick for the period, about 30mm on the front and 14mm everywhere else. The high cost and slow production, and limited combat potential, of the light tank meant that both Vickers and the government

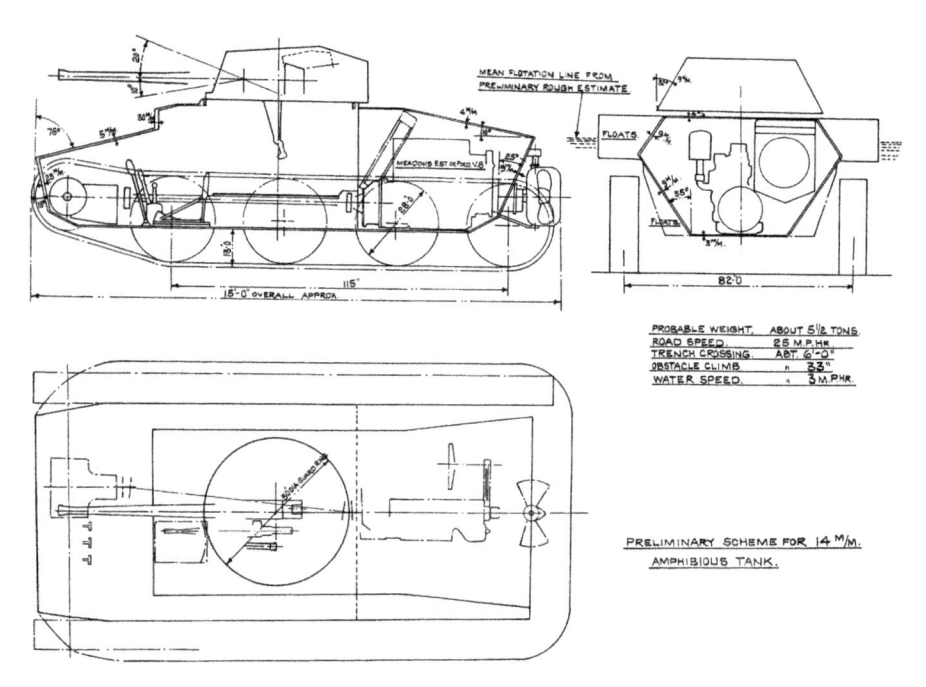

Cutaway of the Vickers proposed 14mm amphibious tank, showing the extremely basic nature of the vehicle.

agreed that this was a bit of a dead end and dropped it before any serious design work took place.

While both these projects were underway, DNLE had carried on working on the AT-1. Their first port of call, in October 1940, had been to carry out some experiments in a naval testing tank, to check water resistance and the wake of the proposed hull. They were also interested in how track propulsion would work and in December 1940 this was investigated. On the latter date, spuds were applied to the tracks, measuring 2-, 1.5- and 1-inch in depth. Even smooth track was calculated. To get a speed of 3 knots, a smooth track would need to be run at a speed of 35mph. The half-inch increments in the spuds produced negligible changes in overall speed: for example, the decrease from 1.5 to 1 inch lost a mere 0.15 knots in speed.

The earlier testing of the hull shape was with a 1/3rd scale model of the hull made with paraffin wax. This was tested in water at speeds from 2 to 6 knots. It was found the fastest practical speed was about 5 knots, as at over 6 knots water resistance increased extremely rapidly. It was found that at 5 knots the bow wave covered the front of the tank but the top hatches were dry. Some hydrodynamic changes were suggested to the hull, such as rounding

The wax tank model undergoing testing, in this case at a speed of 5 knots in still water.

the corners and sprockets of the track. But these were rejected as they would make the tank element of the AT-1 much harder to manufacture and design. The Department for Naval Construction, which was carrying out the tests, idly suggested that paddle wheels be fitted to the tank, and would theoretically get above 5 knots, but it comes as no surprise that these were rejected.

With this data in hand, the DNLE drew up its plans for the AT-1 and submitted them for approval. The War Office requested some changes, the most important of which was the upgrading of the Meadows MAT engine to a Meadows DAV, which increased the AT-1's horsepower from 165 to 250hp. This also meant losing the single-man rear deck machine-gun turret. Another change requested by the War Office was the replacement of the two-man turret with a more standard three-man one. The final request was the addition of suspension; odd as it may seem, the first plans had none. Two versions of the plan were drawn up. The AT-1* had the front wheels sprung while the AT-1** had all its wheels with suspension. The additional weight of the suspension added half a ton to the overall weight. AT-1* was 30.5 tons, while AT-1** weighed in at 31 tons.

The tank's hull was double skinned and with between 40 to 52mm of armour on the front; for 1940 this made it well armoured, which the AT-1 needed. It was a massively tall tank which would have stood out, and been exceptionally hard to take cover with. The rest of the tank had no more than 13.5mm armour, with a roof of 6.5mm. Speed on land was a heady 10mph, and it achieved the required 5 knots at sea.

The crew was five men, an interesting number, as the normal position in contemporary tanks for the fifth man was as the hull machine gunner, a

AT-1** kicking up spray and thrashing through the water during sea trials off Whitmore Bay.

feature not present in the AT-1. The extra crewman, it appears, would have been an engineer to help with the running of the engine in its location deep within the bows of the tank. It is also likely that he would have manned the seacock which was attached to a large ballast tank on the front of the vehicle; when the AT-1 approached land the ballast tank could be flooded to lower the front onto the shore to enable it to grip better.

An order for four tanks, two AT-1* and two AT-1**, was placed with Braithwaites of Newport in March 1941. A series of trials was held from April until October 1942. Those trials, carried out at Barry Island, covered the tank's land performance, which the AT-1 passed, showing a surprising level of mobility for such a large AFV. At Newport docks the tank was winched from the quayside into the water to check that it floated. During this trial it was tethered by a rope to the dockside. Finally, at Whitmore Bay, the AT-1's sea trials were carried out with it sailing under its own power and it was found to have no ability to steer in the water, and to yaw and sheer excessively.

In 1944 three of the AT-1s were scrapped in Cardiff. The fourth vanished. It is possible it may have been gifted to the United States, as they expressed an interest in the project, but no one really knows. Equally no one knows

A pair of images taken at Barry Island, with the AT-1** showing remarkable land performance.

who or what a mysterious AT-1*** was, or how it differed from the original. By now, as Straussler's fabric screen design was progressing and working, and was much cheaper than a specialised tank, the AT-1 found itself on the beach with nowhere to go.

Chapter 4

You Disston my Tank?

In the last part of the 1800s and first decades of the 1900s designers of agricultural machinery wrestled with the same problems that would later necessitate the development of tanks, namely bad terrain. Such agricultural machines were fitted with what we now call tracks, but were then known by a variety of names, normally containing the words 'endless', 'railway', or 'roadway'. An example is the post-First World War company called 'Roadless Traction'.

With a common link between the two types of vehicle, it is no wonder that in dire circumstances people have tried to create tanks out of tractors. The most famous of this type of armoured vehicle was the Bob Semple from New Zealand, described in the *Evening Post* as 'powerful machines'. When first introduced to the public in March 1941 this is what the newspaper had to say:

> as tanks they have immense power. Not only can they climb a grade of 1 in 2, but they will travel through water over four feet deep, traverse an embankment four and a half feet high, smash through gorse hedges, scrub, and saplings up to six inches in diameter, and move across country where roads do not exist. Their armament consists of a number of quick-firing guns. Each tank has a crew of eight, and normally carries 25,000 rounds of ammunition. In addition there is room for the carriage of troops and ammunition in safety over country that might be under enemy fire.

This attempt at public relations failed when the public caught their first glimpse of the Bob Semple. It was an ungainly machine lashed together with whatever materials could be sourced for its armour. The rapid-firing guns were nothing more than machine guns. I suspect the reason this came to epitomise the concept of the armoured tractor is because it looks such a woeful machine, and it has become a good source for a joke.

However before the Bob Semple prejudiced the idea, the armoured tractor was, if not common, then not unknown. Indeed one of the professionally manufactured products from the 1930s seems to have been photographed and inspired by the Bob Semple.

But first we need to travel back to the Russian Civil War. With a mass of competing factions all striving for the upper hand, several armoured tractors were lashed together and thrown into the fighting. Even after the end of the civil war Russia kept on developing the odd design for combat tractors. In July 1941, when the Germans smashed through the borders and the Russian army disintegrated, in a few places newly-built armoured tractors came into being and were used in combat. The sheer number of designs, and the space it would take up, in addition to the fact that details are not readily available to a western historian, means I cannot comment accurately on them.

However, I can talk about the western designs that preceded the Bob Semple. First there was the Sutton Skunk from 1932. It was a US Army surplus 5-ton M1917 Caterpillar tractor, with a lightly armoured body, armed with a pair of machine guns facing forward and, oddly, a pair of mortars firing out of the back of the tank. This vehicle was built at the Disston Works, then possibly shipped to China as part of a sales pitch by its inventor.

The next attempts were two designs that appeared in 1933, although it is difficult to say which was first. One each was designed in the US and the UK.

The British entry came from Richard Garrett and Sons, a company that had existed for 150 years and had pioneered the use of crude-oil (diesel) engines. However, the Great Depression of 1929 hit Garretts hard and in 1932 the company went into receivership. The company was bought by Beyer Peacock, and the factory was renamed the Richard Garrett Engineering Works Ltd, trading on the Garrett name. About the same time that this was happening Garretts had designed and built a tractor for 'trying colonial conditions', as its sales brochure stated. This was called by different names in several places, such as the multi-speed tractor, Garrett pin-track tractor and, in one location, the 'Cormorant'. It was featured in an October 1933 edition of *The Commercial Motor* magazine where the design was attributed to one C.S. Vincent-Smith whom, it is claimed, had been involved in designing tanks for the Army. History does not seem record any details on this designer, or his previous work. However, there is some mystery over the design of the Vickers Medium tanks, which would have been the British Army's standard tank at the time and Vincent-Smith may well have had a hand in that design.

A Garrett multi-speed tractor.

The Garrett tractor weighed about 5.5 tons and could be fitted with a variety of engines, modified as requested by the customer, although the company recommended a Gardner 4L2 engine, producing around 38-50hp. With such an engine fitted, the tractor could reach speeds of 14mph. Larger Gardner engines were also suggested (such as one producing 78hp) and, in a demonstration to the press, a Cormorant fitted with just such a larger engine reached a speed of 20mph. To achieve those speeds the tractor had two gearboxes, one for low speeds where power and torque were needed and the other to provide its top speed.

The engine was mounted on shock absorbers, so that, should the chassis twist or warp during use, there would be no strain on the drive train and the tractor could continue in use. As the engine had an appetite for air it was fitted inside a sealed box with a large air filter to prevent dust entering and destroying the engine. Despite this, attention had been paid to maintenance with the engine being easily accessible. This set-up may have contributed to the tractor's odd shape with the driver at the front with his back against the large engine block.

The suspension was also of novel design with front and rear wheels being mounted on sprung mounts, connected to the inner suspension assemblies, which were then linked to the hull. This would work as a form of automatic track-tension system.

A Garrett tractor showing off the unique way its track worked, and the large range of motion within the suspension arms.

With the financial crisis affecting the entire world, the idea for mounting an armoured body on the tractor was sold as an advantage. On one hand you had a tractor capable of doing normal tractor-related activities, but should your army or police force need some armoured support you could fit an armoured body onto the tractor. After the need had vanished you could remove the body and have the tractor back. The idea was this should offer substantial savings for a hard-pressed government. The fact that the cheapness was looked at can be seen from the sales pamphlet which pointed out each set of tracks only cost £35 (about £2,000 today) and the entire tractor could be shipped anywhere in the world in a wooden crate, with the exact dimensions and weights listed, allowing the purchaser to work out what transportation would cost.

One final advantage of the Cormorant chassis was that it could neutral steer. This ability to rotate on the spot was considered an advantage in the tank role for internal security.

With the tank body fitted, there was a crew of three with the driver in the middle and, to either side of him, a gunner who could operate the weapons. What weapons were to be fitted was again left up to the requirements of the

YOU DISSTON MY TANK?

The Garrett demonstrating its neutral steer capability. A top-down view, taken during the same demonstration, is shown on the next page.

customer, but one could easily imagine any machine gun in the openings. Another six men, or stores, could be carried inside the hull with the passengers sitting on the bonnet of the engine, although the space would seem to be very cramped, and lacked headroom. The body itself was of 6mm armour plate and was claimed to stand up to a .303 bullet at any range. There were doors on the side of the hull and at the rear of the tank, plus hatches on the roof. The roof was sloped to throw off grenades. The sales pamphlet also pointed out that the tracks could be damaged by enemy fire, but still run. Despite all these good points, it seems that not one country brought the armoured body.

The other 1933 entry into the 'armoured tractor' market was the more successful armoured body produced by Disston. Unlike the Garrett, the Disston started life incorporating a real cannon. The gun in question was a short 37mm gun, possibly an M1916 infantry gun. The hull had a ball-mounted Browning machine gun. There were two versions of the vehicle, one with the gun on a pedestal mount, the other with it in the turret. It is not known which came first, but the only models sold overseas were turreted. Pictures show a further variant which generally looks like the turretless version, although the sides of the hull have been built up to provide increased protection for the gunner.

The chassis chosen for this conversion was the Caterpillar 35. Released in 1932, it also came with a choice of engines, including a diesel. The tractor itself weighed in at around six to seven tons but was of a much more conventional design in track style and layout with the driver at the rear.

YOU DISSTON MY TANK?

The Garrett tank, possibly at the Garret works in Leiston, Suffolk.

The tractor with armoured body itself could only reach 6.5mph. Cost was quoted at about $21,000 Canadian dollars (about $300,000 today) per unit. Unlike the Garrett the Caterpillar enjoyed much more success in the sales market in both armoured and unarmoured forms although one would guess that armoured versions would not have had the distinctive bright yellow Caterpillar colour.

Four of the Afghanistan Disstons. The tank nearest the camera lacks its main gun.

Unfortunately, at this time exact details of sales for the armoured version are not known but most of the sales seem to have been in 1935. Some were offered to Canada to arm their army in spring 1935 but were rejected because of their poor speed. China had sixteen on order but also cancelled, again in 1935.

There are also rumours of a number being supplied to the US Marine Corps in 1933, but no evidence to back this up has been found, although in 1935 the USMC got hold of more armour in the shape of CTL-1 tanks. Finally, we have the one real user. Afghanistan used a number of Disstons from 1935. Photographs of the Disstons in service all appear to be the turreted design. It might be that the Afghan AFVs were ex-USMC although that is conjecture, and should be treated as such. The Afghan Disston order may also have included a number of bodies to be fitted to the tractor units, a task which took about two hours. At the time Afghanistan was a slowly modernizing society, which caused some friction amongst tribal leaders, so the Disston tractors may well have seen action against such foes, although details of any combat use are non-existent. Afghanistan may also be the last place on earth where you can see a Disston. At least one was preserved at the national museum, and then, after the Western invasion, it and other Disstons ended up at a Kabul scrapyard. Those bodies may still be there, awaiting retrieval, or they may already have met their fate.

In 1936 the Spanish Civil War broke out and, as is often the case, poorly-equipped forces have to make do with improvised armoured vehicles.

The Italian-built Colqualber moving across the Ethiopian countryside.

It is likely that several tractors were armed and armoured and used in this bitter conflict.

Possibly the last non-Russian contender in the armoured tractor story is in Africa. In July 1941 two tractors were converted by the Italians to try to retain their hold on Ethiopia, which they had captured in 1936. For use against joint British and Ethiopian forces, the Italians protected two tractors, both made by Caterpillar. Both vehicles were named after the locations where they were presumably built and served, Volchefit and Culqualber. The first was a Caterpillar RD7 fitted with 75hp engine. The later was a Caterpillar D6 with a 65hp engine, Volchefit, bristled with 6.5mm M.14 machine guns, mounting seven such weapons. Culqualber was much more modestly armed with two 8mm M14/M35 machine guns. Protection was provided by metal planks, made from leaf springs for trucks. The overall impression from photographs is that of a shed lurching over the ground. But with even such an ungainly machine as these Italian conversions, or the Bob Semple, one point stands out. When used against lightly-armed enemies, with no heavy weapons, any protected mobile machine gun is useful as long as one remembers its limitations, a lesson often forgotten by British officers when dealing with Universal carriers.

Chapter 5

The Smoking Gun

In the 1920s the British started looking at the problem of anti-tank guns and how they would affect tanks on the battlefield. It was quickly realised that the tanks needed some way of closing with the enemy while not being destroyed by the enemy's anti-tank guns. The obvious idea was to block the enemy's line of sight with smoke. Normally smoke would be provided by artillery but artillery was relatively imprecise and took time to deploy. What was needed was a smoke capability that could be provided organically to the tank unit. The problem for the British was that their normal guns only fired solid shot and were intended for anti-tank work. They could create a shell that was filled with smoke and fire it from the same gun, but the actual smoke coverage would be insignificant and of limited use. This was due to the relatively high velocity the anti-tank guns produced and the small projectile, limiting the size of the projectile's payload. What the War Office envisioned was a large shell fired at low velocity. Providing one such gun on each tank, as well as the main weapon, would be expensive and impractical and thus the idea of a 'close support' (CS) tank was born. At first there was an idea that the close support tank would be a lighter, less complicated and, most importantly, cheaper vehicle which could carry seventy rounds of ammunition. It was sometimes referred to as the 'artillery tank'. This line of thought may have been tied in with the development of the Birch gun of the mid-1920s but, in due course, it was seen as a better, and cheaper, idea to fit the new gun into a small number of normal tanks within the unit, without needing the separate logistics and tooling required to produce a unique vehicle.

By the early 1920s a gun had been developed to fulfil the close support role, and was fitted, with some work, into a Vickers Medium Mk I. Of 3.7-inch calibre, the gun is often confused with the First World War mountain howitzer of the same calibre or, at least, suggested to be a development of it. In truth, it appears to have had absolutely no links to the earlier piece, and was an entirely new gun. It fired a 15lb shell and, to enable a high rate of fire, it was given a semi-automatic breech.

A pair of Vickers Medium Mk IIA close support tanks in Egypt.

On a normal quick-firing gun the breech needs to be manually closed but a semi-automatic breech will automatically close when a shell is inserted. It was found that if this happened and the gunner still had the firing handle compressed the gun would fire, while the loader's left hand was still practically touching the breech. This would have the obvious result of a smashed arm and was therefore considered too dangerous.

It was also found that the rate of fire required was not as high as the designers of the gun had anticipated. Firing tests showed that one or two rounds a minute would produce a suitable smokescreen. In one test firing, while the tank was moving, six rounds were fired over four minutes that masked a large area. In another test, two rounds screened an area of about 800 square yards.

The shell itself used charged smoke, which is today known as white phosphorus. A list of ammunition types gives the round designations as being called 'smoke', 'charged smoke' and 'high explosive'. It is important to note that official documents do actually call the shell 'high explosive'. This is where that British eccentricity rears up. The 'smoke' and 'charged smoke' were pretty much identical, both with the same sized bursting charge and carrying 2lbs 5oz of white phosphorus.

No example has been discovered of an HE round being used from the gun. It appears that the 'HE' shell had a slightly larger bursting charge

The screening effect resulting from of a rapid barrage of ten rounds.

(1oz 12dr) for added 'morale effect on enemy troops' but otherwise functioned exactly as a smoke shell. It also carried a smaller white phosphorus payload, weighing in at 1lb 11oz. A Royal Artillery officer was invited to view a test of the shell but his one-page report is very

Comparisons between the two types of shell. The effect of the 'HE' shell is in the top picture, and smoke in the bottom. As you can see they are all but identical in effect.

damning. He explained in no uncertain terms what a bad idea this was, describing the idea as laughable, and pointing out that such a small charge would barely be noticeable on the battlefield.

The gun itself was built in two versions. However, the mark designation was only used within the Royal Tank Corps to designate between the two guns which caused all sorts of confusion and reproachful letters between civil servants and military officers.

The unofficial Royal Tank Corps system was fairly simple. The prototype weapon with the semi-automatic breech and unique mounting which could only be fitted to a Vickers Medium Mk I was termed the Mk I. The production version, with the normal breech and a universal mounting, became the Mk II. Part of the reason for this unofficial naming system was that, in 1923, the original Mk I Vickers Medium close support tank was delivered to Lulworth. This was one of the first two Vickers Mediums delivered and, for the next seven years, the Royal tank Corps only had that one tank to play with. For some unknown reason, they took that long before producing their final report.

By the time the Mk II came out, the gun had been altered significantly to allow it to be totally interchangeable with the 3-pounder gun then used in the Vickers Medium tanks. All that was needed was to swap out the gun

A formation of Mk I and Mk IA Vickers Medium tanks on parade for an exercise. The two lead tanks, and the seventh (far right of picture) have been detailed to stand in as 'close support' tanks, painted with white barrels and the designation 'CS'.

and the range drum. This design took years to perfect but, by August 1931, the first Mk II guns had passed proof and two had been issued to the Tank Gunnery School at Lulworth.

The desire for the equipment was there, although, as pictures of Vickers Mediums on exercise indicate, you will often see tanks with their guns painted white and the letters 'CS' on the turret sides to denote a close support tank. Equally a 1925 organisation issued by the War Office required every tank battalion to have three CS tanks. Of course, there seems an obvious answer to the delay: there simply was not the money for it. With no chance of a major war in Europe, no need was seen for it. It could be that the government only started looking in seriousness at the CS gun for the Medium Mk II, and did development work from there. All the documents I have found so far are dated later than 1928.

A flurry of work was done towards the end of the 1920s. Then in September 1931 each tank battalion was issued one gun. The slow pace of issue carried on until the units were up to full complement. In 1933 a slight problem was noticed by the civil servants. The name of the gun was very similar to that of the 3.7-inch mountain howitzer used by the infantry. So an official proclamation was issued: henceforth the gun would be known as the QF 3.7-inch tank mortar.

One of the first Vickers Medium tanks, in its Mk I CS guise, at Bloemfontein Barracks.

The story of tanks in South Africa between the wars is a very short one. First you have 'His Majesty's Landship Union', a Medium Mk A Whippet that was used mainly as a propaganda tool, although during strikes in 1922 it was used to support the government forces. Its début was a bit dismal and it got bogged down on a street. While dismounted its driver was killed by a sniper.

Then in 1933 the South African government approached the British to ask for a tank capable of mounting a 3.7-inch gun capable of firing tear-gas shells. A round was duly designed and tested. However, it was a failure with the sticky tear-gas gell failing to ignite. Despite this, two close support tanks were shipped to South Africa in August 1934. These were Medium Mk I models and at least one of them had had very hard life. It was one of the earliest Medium Mk I tanks produced and had been used as a test bed for a new very powerful engine. It had so much power that the lowest gear had to be disabled. To fit this monstrous engine, most of the front hull was heavily modified. After the trials it was returned to its normal configuration and used as an instructional hull at Bovington before it and its sister were gifted to the South Africans. One of the pair survives as a gate guardian at Bloemfontein Barracks.

The other change in 1934 was a round of modifications and all the mortars were withdrawn from service, apart from one gun in Egypt. Then the document trail disappears for a few years and the next time we encounter the tank mortar is as the gun on the A.9 and A.10 Cruiser tanks in the run up to and in the first years of the Second World War.

The combat records for a tank that can only fire smoke are difficult to find, and so the tank mortar passes into history. However, to give an idea of what the tank mortar would have been like in combat there is the following short account. The unit in question was equipped with Crusaders, and would have been using the 3-inch howitzer for the CS role, but the fight would have gone much the same anywhere the tank mortar was used.

In the retreat to El Alamein, the officer commanding the squadron spotted some suspicious vehicles moving behind him. He drew his tanks up in a semi-circle pointing towards the possible enemy. While he called it into his regimental commander, the crews of the tanks observed the oncoming dust-cloud, looking for a clue as to whom the vehicles belonged to. Then permission was given to open fire. Four tanks of the squadron headquarters were CS tanks. On order, they began firing as fast as they could, the shells drawing a line of smoke across the bright blue desert sky. After four volleys, the twelve gun-armed Crusaders moved out, gathering speed and heading right for the billowing smoke bank. As they drew closer the tanks disappeared into the cloud of smoke. Through the clouds flashes of gunfire could be seen and, shortly afterwards, the thump of the guns could be heard. After about ten minutes, silence descended on the battlefield, then shapes could be seen moving. Slowly they resolved themselves into the Crusaders that had launched the attack. As they closed back to the start line, they swung about and reformed their semi-circular position.

Chapter 6

Hail Hydran!

Tiny engineering companies sprang up all over the place in the first half of the twentieth century. Some made it big and expanded into the giant companies with names we all recognise, but many are lost to history. One such company was Hydran Products Ltd. This company sticks in my mind simply because of the work of one of its designers, Mr Lewis Motley.

I cannot provide many details about either the company or Mr Motley, as this information is lost, but I know both their addresses, as these are listed on their patents: Hydran Products was based at the Hydra Works, Gresham Road, Staines. Mr Motley's address was at Clapham Common, some seventeen miles away, so he had a daily commute of about an hour, assuming the Germans had not bombed the railway he was to use. The earliest mention of Hydran Products was in 1937 when they started producing oil burners to provide heat, which were still used decades later. This seems to have been their most successful product until the war broke out. The company left several ideas and patents from the war years, all stemming from Motley's remarkable imagination.

The first entry is in 1940 when Hydran Products designed a new belt-feed system for the Ministry of Aviation and its Hispano 20mm cannon. Hydran Products was also asked to design and build 3,750 mountings for twin Vickers heavy machine guns to be used in the AA role. The company was responsible for the very common Motley mounts that came in five versions (Marks 1 to 5). These enabled one or two Bren guns to be mounted in the AA role, and served in every theatre of the war in some numbers. Some mounts were trialled with Browning .303 machine guns. The production of the mounts was, I suspect, the majority of the company's war work.

However, in July 1942 Mr Motley submitted an ambitious design to the gunnery school at Lulworth. It consisted of a Universal carrier with thicker armour to the front of the vehicle. On the rear, mounted on the engine deck, was a turntable with four 6-pounder gun barrels fitted; each barrel was pre-loaded and sealed at the breech end. The round inside the

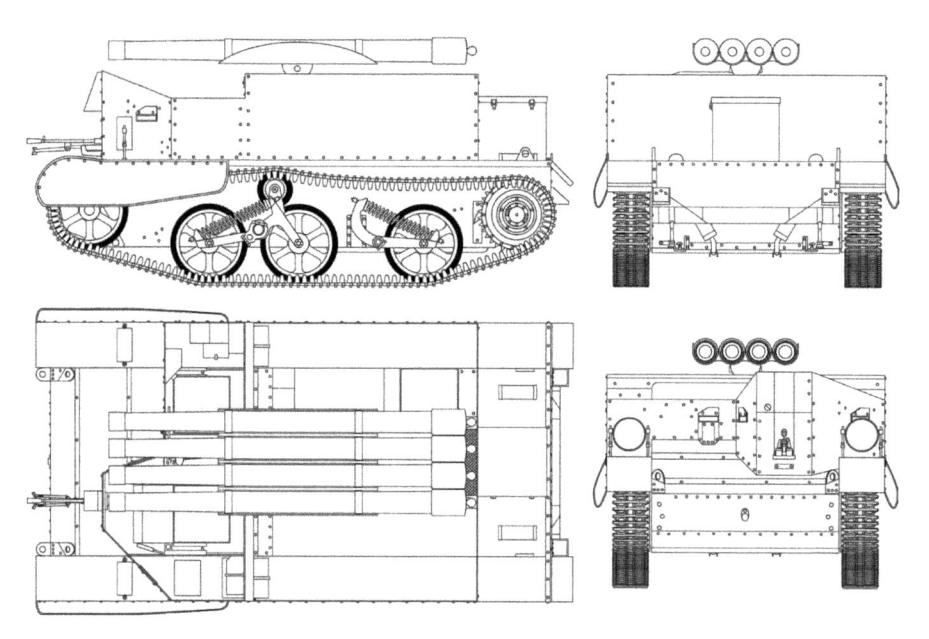

Plan of a Motley modified carrier with its tray of 6-pounder barrels.

gun was fired electrically and, to absorb the recoil, the entire barrel flew off the back of the carrier. After the four tubes had been fired the carrier would retire to reload.

Motley envisioned the carriers approaching at high speed and making attack runs in the manner of motor torpedo boats against larger ships. After all, if you have cruiser tanks in the desert, why not MTB tanks?

Mr Motley's next invention appeared in 1944, when he seems to have found out about rockets, and turned his mind to their use. He designed a rocket gun with a selectable rate of fire like an assault rifle and, on 4 April 1944, submitted his patent. The gun was fed from the top, with each rocket projectile dropping down into the breech. The gun had one flaw in its design: if the previous rocket failed to launch the next round would explode in the breach and the soldier manning the weapon, when the round launched, would suffer the full blast of the rocket motor.

To combat this Mr Motley submitted another patent on 17 July, in which he launched a liquid-fuel rocket with a gunpowder charge. Once away from the barrel the rocket would ignite. In May 1945 he submitted a similar patent for the same principle with solid-fuel rockets.

By December 1944 he was ready with another patent, this time to combat the problem of the exploding gun if there was a failure to launch.

HAIL HYDRAN!

An artist's impression of a British soldier armed with the Motley rocket gun and, below, the plans based upon the patents filed by Mr Motley during 1944 and 1945.

The solution was a large drum, with a timing shoe at the muzzle. During launch, the rocket pressed the timing shoe, allowing the next chamber to move into position, and so could only be fired when the barrel was clear.

After this Motley carried on working on the ideas for rockets, submitting patents for a worm-drive loader, feeding from multiple magazines to save space, in April 1945, a belt feed for rocket loading with each belt holding 100 rockets in June and, finally, in November, a method of loading using something akin to the blowback principle.

The only patent that can be found for Motley after the Second World War concerns street lighting, and Mr Motley and Hydran Products disappear from the historical record.

Chapter 7

The Cambridge Camal

Towards the end of the Second World War, the British Ordnance Board issued a requirement for a new infantry support gun of extremely light weight. While lightweight guns existed, such as the German *Leichtes Infanteriegeschütz* 18, which weighed in at 880lb complete, they were mounted on a full-sized carriage which accounted for a substantial portion of the weight. The War Office was asking for something that was truly lightweight, as the requirement was for a gun that could be carried by two men. Conventional guns and shells made this difficult, if not impossible, to achieve. Luckily, research into new ammunition was producing new possibilities. One of those concepts opened the way to meeting the requirements.

The shell in question was the Cambridge Projectile. The exact start date of its development is not recorded, but it was probably sometime in 1942 or early 1943. The idea behind it was to design a flame weapon with much longer range than a normal flame-thrower. To achieve this, the shell needed to have a high capacity and, of course, the highest capacity projectile is a cylinder. This cylinder was then filled with flammable liquid. However, rotating a cylinder of liquid, as with a traditional shell to give it the required stability for long-range accuracy, will make it very unstable due to centrifugal forces. So the decision was taken to fire it from a smoothbore weapon. Of course, a blunt-nosed shell fired from a smoothbore will also be horribly unstable in flight and thus very inaccurate but it was discovered that, if the sheath of unstable air was brought behind the centre of gravity, the shell would then become stable enough to get the required long-range accuracy.

During development the weapon designers, possibly the Petroleum Warfare Department, were aiming for accuracy at extremely long ranges. It was at that point that the obvious occurred: a satisfactory degree of accuracy at long range means that, at much closer ranges, accuracy would be extremely good. This, combined with the Cambridge shell's high capacity, meant that it had a number of envisioned uses, such as flame, incendiary, smoke, chemical warfare, hollow-charge, and low-shrapnel high-explosive.

So, with a clear advantage and having overcome the main disadvantage normally associated with a blunt-nosed shell, the rounds moved on to the testing stage. It was found that the shells would often deform at the base when firing due to the pressures but these problems were solved in short order. Rounds for the 3-inch mortar were developed and tested but, despite the advantage in payload, the amount of material was still insufficient for a suitable flame shell.

To carry out further trials a simple smoothbore gun was constructed. The original shell design was made of impregnated Bakelite paper filled with thickened petrol and white phosphorus. The simple nature of the test weapon may be grasped by the fact that the Cambridge shell did not have a cartridge case, and so the gun could not be depressed, lest the round fall out, although production shells did have a cartridge case.

Recoil from this trials gun was managed by it having a very heavy steel barrel of around 200lb and a pair of small springs to deal with the remainder of the recoil.

In July 1943 trials were carried out with a round for a 3-inch howitzer, of the same type mounted on the Churchill I and the Matilda CS tanks. It is

The test gun, with its heavy smoothbore steel barrel.

THE CAMBRIDGE CAMAL

A Vickers Medium Mk I, engulfed in a cloud of white phosphorus after a Cambridge shell hits it on the rear hull.

interesting to note that both these and the later 75mm guns were rifled, yet the very principle of the round needed it to be fired unrotated.

As the 3-inch howitzer was obsolete by this stage of the war, twenty-two rounds were manufactured for the Royal Ordnance 75mm. Major Hyslop of the Petroleum Warfare Department asked the Canadian army to lend them a 75mm armed tank on 6 October 1943 with the aim of conducting the 75mm testing later in the month. For some reason, comparative trials against normal rotated 75mm shells only happened in May 1944. The Cambridge shell was considerably more accurate up to 2,500 yards, and was lighter and had a higher payload than a normal 75mm round.

The requirement for the lightweight infantry gun appeared in January 1945 and asked for a weapon that could be towed or man-packed, by a minimum of two soldiers, with no single load exceeding 100lb, and a maximum gun crew of four. This, of course, meant the maximum weight of the complete weapon could only be 200lb.

The role of the equipment specified in the requirement was for a platoon level weapon to keep enemy tanks away and prevent them from bringing effective small-arms fire onto the infantry. The reason for its lightness was so that it could keep up with the infantry in terrain that would prevent normal anti-tank guns being brought up, such as if the infantry crossed an anti-tank obstacle or penetrated a minefield. Minimum range was to be 500 yards, at which range the weapon had to be able to hit a stationary 5-feet-square target or a moving 5-feet-high by 15-feet-long target, moving at 10mph. Rate of fire was to be at least five aimed rounds per minute. The reason for the range of 500 yards was that this was judged to be the maximum a weapon could be used without complex optical sights such as a telescope, although an optical sight was desired for long-range fire.

The gun built to test fire the Cambridge shell was used as a starting point. The new gun design was called the 'Camal gun', or, in one entry in the documents, the 'Cam-Al gun'. This was presumably due to the abbreviations of Cambridge, 'Cam', and AL, 'aluminium'. It also harks back to the lightweight portability that resembled camel guns from previous centuries.

The heavy steel barrel was replaced by one made of RR77 aluminium alloy with a weight one third that of steel. The majority of the gun was made from this alloy. For comparison, the aluminium barrel's weight had dropped from 200lb down to only 47lb.

The recoil was managed by adding an oil-type recuperator, slightly modified and taken from a Vickers S gun, while the breech was an interrupted screw type. Even so, the recoil was too great to allow it to be fired on a tripod giving 360-degree arc of fire, and so they had to settle for the minimum in the requirement which was an arc of 90 degrees. The final version of the mount had a tripod with two long rear legs and a shorter front

The completed lightweight Camal gun prototype, ready to be moved into production.

Cambridge 3 inch HEAT (left) and HE (right) rounds.

leg; the requirement also called for it to be towable. As a result, the mount was designed so that the front leg could be removed and replaced with a simple axle and two light car wheels, while the longer rear legs closed together to become the towing bar. Once it arrived at its destination the axle and wheels could be unlatched and the normal leg fitted.

The main aim of the gun was destruction of enemy tanks. High-explosive anti-tank shells perform much better when unrotated, so it was obvious this type of shell would be selected. A Royal Ordnance 95mm HEAT cone was cut down to fit the dimensions of the 3-inch Cambridge shell and the round tested. In the first test the Cambridge HEAT shell went clean through

120mm of armour at 30 degrees. A second test later achieved penetration of 150mm plate at 30 degrees. To give an idea of what this means on the battlefield, such a performance would likely penetrate the frontal armour of a Panther. In comparison the full-sized 95mm round would only penetrate 110mm plate at 30 degrees.

Muzzle velocity of the shell was recorded as 710 feet per second (fps) and, with 5 degrees of elevation on the gun barrel, the round travelled 818 yards. In addition, high explosive and white phosphorus shells were developed for the gun. However, as the Second World War was coming to a close, and man-portable recoilless weapons were coming more common, it seems that the Camal gun development was halted, and the weapon faded from history.

Chapter 8

Schwimmpanzer 36

On 26 February 1936 a report was filed by the British intelligence agencies about some alarming information coming out of Germany on the development of amphibious tanks. The report caught the British by surprise as at the time the only tank type the Germans were known to own was the Panzer I.

The report described several incidents of amphibious tanks collected from sources throughout Austria and Germany. In the first report in 1932 an Austrian source said that the Germans had built a very good amphibious tank, and that two versions of it were in store at Kummersdorf. During the next two years, continued reports came out about an amphibious tank designed by the German equivalent of the British War Office. These reports named the firms involved, Krupp, MAN, Bussing and Magirus. Then, suddenly, all mention of the vehicle stopped and it seemed to drop out of sight.

Then in 1935 a report arrived of the *Kriegsmarine* carrying out tests at Kiel of an amphibious tank that travelled 1.5 miles to shore from its launching point. This report gave the vehicle's statistics: it was described as 6.5 tons in weight, with 22mm of armour and propelled by a 75hp engine, giving it a top speed of 28mph. Dimensions were listed as 20.5 feet in length. A 47mm gun and machine gun were mounted in a turret, and it had a crew of five.

Both the screw and rudder were under armour, and the tank could switch to water mode in about five minutes without the crew needing to leave the vehicle. It was also described as a wheel-cum-track machine.

Upon reading the performance of the vehicle the British were intrigued, and a little worried! At the time the standard British tank was the Vickers Medium Mk II, although the Medium Mk III had been tested. This strange Panzer had better armour, the same fire-power, was faster and amphibious, all in a smaller package. However, not everyone was convinced with one technical expert saying:

> It is surprising that these tanks are also wheel-cum-track machines as this adds extra complication and weight in addition to the screw and rudder.

The length of 20 feet 6 inches is greater than one would expect of a 6-ton tank and the 22mm of armour could only be in a few places around the turret.

If the data given is correct then the tanks must be a wonderful achievement in design.

Frankly we do not believe that this information is correct in every detail.

With modern research we can actually make a good guess as to what this tank actually was. It also highlights, I believe, the difference between reality and the strange world in which intelligence departments live.

First the tank was actually an armoured car and hence the confusion about the wheel-cum-track. Even then, the number of road wheels was wrong with ten being reported, but the real vehicle having only eight.

The mysterious vehicle was, I think, the very German named *Mannschaftstransportwagen I*, from now on referred to by its initials 'MTW'.

There are several facts that link the reports to the MTW. The vehicle was first designed in the very late 1920s, had a five-man crew, a turret with a 37mm gun, and the screw was under armour. One of the reports states that it was powered by a 100hp engine.

Russian and German soldiers surround the *Mannschaftstransportwagen* at the Soviet-German testing area at Kazan.

Equally the list of firms, while not a perfect match, does have some similarities, especially the involvement of Magirus. The armour, however, was wrong; the MTW had 13.5mm all the way round. That is nonetheless still better than British tanks of the period. One reason for these discrepancies is that the source that was supplying the information would not have had time to measure or take notes but would have had to guess and then remember.

For me the final proof is the fact the MTW seemed to disappear for a while. According to various sources, it was in Russia being put through its tests, then returned to Germany for more tests, where it was spotted and at least semi-correct details were passed on to the British.

Chapter 9

Recoil Control

One of the biggest problems in gun manufacture is that of recoil. A great many inventors have tried to develop ways of managing it, such as the Jones-Wise projector, or recoilless rifles like the Bazooka, which use a back-blast to counter some of the recoil.

As I have mentioned the Jones-Wise projector, I would quickly like to touch upon its unique design, as not many details, or even a picture of it, seem to have survived. It was first brought to Prime Minister Winston Churchill's attention in October 1940. Designed by a pair of Home Guard officers, the Royal Navy tested the weapon, as did the Army, but both turned it down, the Royal Navy because they deferred in the matters of anti-tank weapons to the Army. The Army turned it down because the Home Guard had Northover projectors and the devastating Blacker Bombards while the Smith Gun was just coming into service. It was felt that another anti-tank weapon was surplus to requirements. The weapon was called a 'Heath Robinson contraption' by one officer who saw it and described it as a semi-circular trough with a parallel sighting bar, shaped like a rifle, with sights on top. Into the trough, a steel tube, which acted as the barrel, was loaded, containing a round of ammunition. Upon firing, the round was discharged forwards, and the barrel propelled backwards, which made the weapon ready to take another shot instantly with no recoil. The problem, of course, was that the steel tube weighed 34lb, and was flying backwards at a high rate of speed which would be incredibly dangerous to friendly soldiers. Since the entire mass was the gun's barrel, each round would need a new barrel. Thus, while the actual gun was cheap to produce, the ammunition would be expensive.

To fire the gun one of the crew members had to strike a cartridge sticking out of the barrel with a hand-held hammer, which would make fine aiming and shots against a moving target extremely difficult.

After the First World War a pair of Frenchmen, one of whom was called M. Galliot, while the other's name is given as Borg or Bory, were working on a new muzzle brake, which created a backblast to reduce recoil. Unlike a recoilless rifle, this could be fitted to any normal gun. In 1919 experiments were held in the USA and, in 1924, the results of the experiments were submitted to the US authorities. The muzzle brake worked by directing the expanding gases that propel the projectile backwards through a series of fluted spiral channels. Tests found that there were two pressure waves a few milliseconds apart, with a third lower down as the blast reflected off the ground. It was an incredibly complex piece of equipment that at least two government departments refused point-blank to consider manufacturing due to its complexity.

After the fall of France in 1940, Galliot, by then a commandant, ended up in the UK and the first attempts were made to fit a Galliot muzzle brake to rifles. In 1941 it was fitted to a 6-pounder and, during 1942, there were several trials with the weapon but, while the recoil was reduced by 81 per cent, the backblast was tremendous. A redesign of the gun mounts was required so that they could survive the pressure waves. On 5 August 1943 trials were carried out on a 17-pounder mounted on a normal carriage while repeat trials on 6 October had the gun mounted on a Lorraine 37L. A Renault UE was also pictured with the 6-pounder mounted on it but the source of the French vehicles has always been a bit of a mystery. There are suggestions that about seventeen Renault

The Renault UE and Lorraine 37L with the guns and Galliot muzzle brakes fitted.

RECOIL CONTROL

Side shot of the Lorraine 37L with the fine details of the Galliot design visible.

UEs reached Britain after the fall of France, but no sources mention the Lorraine 37L.

During the trials on a carriage, the front ring on the muzzle brake cracked on the first round and after two rounds the ring was removed. In total, six rounds were fired, and ten rounds during the trial mounted on the Lorraine.

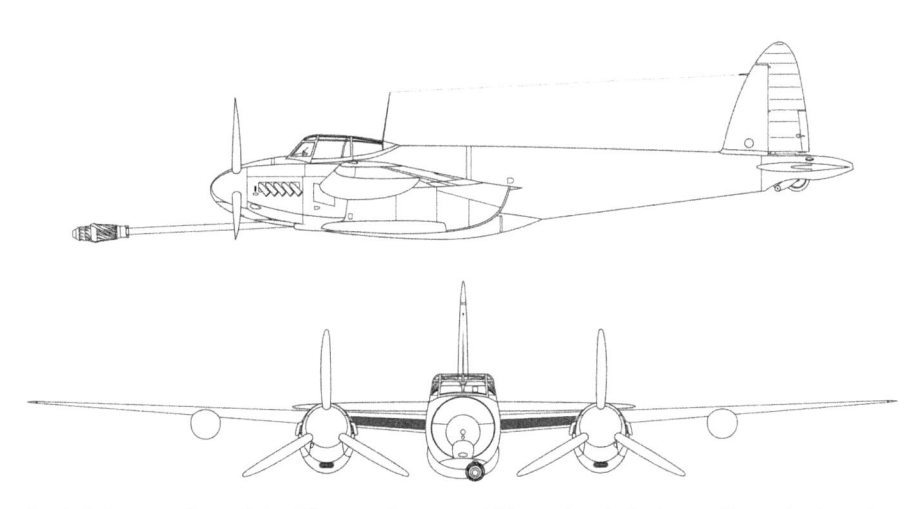

Artist's impression of the 32-pounder armed Mosquito. It is drawn from the location of the sensors during the trials. These were matched to points on the aircraft and airframe drawn from there.

During the trials on the 17-pounder pressure sensors were placed around the gun, including two at the locations where the ears of the gun-layer would be, and some directly under the muzzle brake. At a range of just over four feet, the pressure peak nearly reached the minimum levels needed to rupture the human lung. Equally concerning, at the ears of the gun-layer the threshold was reached for eardrum rupture. Higher peak pressures were recorded about six feet from the side of the vehicle, which was farther back than the gun-layer. For the reasons of crew safety, development was not continued.

Then came the idea of fitting the Galliot muzzle brake to a Mosquito FB XVIII (Tsetse). Later it was suggested that the Tsetse be re-armed with a 32-pounder gun. Trials were carried out on 14 August 1945 with a single gun on a ground mount placed at a height of 6 feet 9 inches, at an angle of 5 degrees. Sensors were placed to conform with the locations corresponding to the tip of the nose and spinner hub, and the edges of the propeller blade discs on a normal Mosquito Tsetse. Exact details on the results are unclear, but there is a suggestion this aircraft was actually built and flown, although no archive material has been found to confirm this.

Chapter 10

The Soldierless Tank

In the early 1930s the British Army and the Royal Navy worked together on remotely-controlled ships. One such project was fitting coastal motor boats with radio control, although it was never completed. Another that was completed by Mr Evershed of the Royal Navy Signals School was the fitting of the old battleship HMS *Centurion** with remote control to use it as a target drone for coastal artillery batteries.

HMS *Centurion* during her time as a coastal artillery target vessel.

---

* HMS *Centurion* ended her days by being sunk at Arromanches on 9 June 1944 as part of the breakwater for the British Mulberry harbour, Port Winston.

From that basis the idea of a remotely-controlled tank on land grew. The first hint of such a tank was in October 1935. Since the Air Ministry had more experience with radios and electronics than the Army, the Army enquired if they knew of any reason why a remote-control tank would not work up to a distance of two miles from its control station. With the Air Ministry's positive reply, the Army proposed to set up a conference on the subject and initiate a joint project.

There is some debate as to who came up with the idea of the remote-control tank. Brigadier Percy Hobart made the claim that it was his idea, but that is based entirely upon a minute in a 1937 meeting being deleted. A review into the UK records conducted in 1946 suggests that the idea came from an officer called Chapham, but fails to credit him with his full name or rank.

On 5 December 1935 the first meeting on the subject was held and the basic role of a remotely-controlled tank was defined:

1. To carry out reconnaissance of an area over which an attack may be made. The idea of the remote-control tank was to draw fire from enemy guns, so that they could be targeted.
2. To find out the location of enemy minefields by driving into them and, finally, to be used as a mobile mine. The explosive charge could also be used to destroy the tank should it be in danger of being captured. A requirement was that it should be controllable from a standard issue army radio set.

The project was codenamed 'Edward'.

Upon hearing the requirements, the Air Ministry declared that it would probably take two years to develop. Then both departments of the Air Ministry present at the conference started using it as a chance to empire build. The Royal Aircraft Establishment demanded an increase in staffing levels, while the Air Ministry itself asked for an extra £5,000 in its budget, to be taken from the Army's budget. In 1936 the project was regulated to minor status by the Air Ministry, as they had several of their own projects, although those were mostly remote-control aircraft such as the de Havilland Queen Bee. Of the £5,000 allocated to the Air Ministry only £708 of the grant had been spent on Edward, of which £638 was for the gearbox.

Initial testing had found that an automatic gearbox was needed. One had been designed by Freeborn Power Converters Ltd and fitted to an omnibus, on which it had completed 28,000 miles without fault.

With the gearbox problem solved the rest of the tank was needed. In the end a light tank Mk II was used, and fitted with a Rolls Royce engine. The hull was modified with two bulges on the glacis plate to hold steering linkages while, internally, an automatic starter was installed.

In July 1936 the Air Ministry announced that its projects were finished and that it would need £4,880 for 1937 to work on Edward. Once again the Army paid, but work was moving forward and, in February 1937, a problem with the steering control was solved. By this time, however, the Army was getting restless. With its budget going missing and no apparent results, Colonel Giffard le Q. Martel sent a very strongly worded series of letters enquiring how the project was progressing. The Air Ministry managed to placate the Army by pointing out that, by May, the radio equipment was working well under laboratory conditions. However, the mechanical side of things was not going so well. The brakes were far too powerful, slamming full on as soon as they were engaged. Conversely, the servos powering the gear selection and the track drives were too weak. Nonetheless, the Air Ministry announced that Edward would be complete in three to six months.

A Vickers Light tank Mk II being prepared for photographing in 1931. It lacks the Edward modifications.

Edward was demonstrated privately on 1 June 1936, and pronounced ready for full demonstrations on 2 July. Those demonstrations did not take place until the following year. During the demonstrations, held on 13 January 1937, those present were very impressed by the performance of Edward, despite the brake problem. A question was raised about Edward's future. In the previous year Edward had switched from being a project for service to being a technology demonstrator. The visiting dignitaries asked where the research project could go from its current high point. One suggestion was to use Edward as target for anti-tank gunner training.

In light of its flawless performance Edward was given a stay of execution. Some additional goals were added, to increase the range of operation up to 3,000 yards, the ability to lay a smoke screen (which resulted in an air compressor being fitted) and a safety system that would stop the tank if it did not receive a signal for more than 30 seconds. Trials at Bovington were scheduled for later that year, and Edward returned to being a project for a piece of service equipment. The Air Ministry asked for another £5,200 to cover development in 1938, which was approved on Christmas Eve 1937.

In late 1937 the Army was developing its new radio set, the No. 11, which would give the added range needed to reach 3,000 yards control; thus it was tested with Edward. Almost immediately, Edward developed its own consciousness, sometimes driving around under its own control ignoring the signals from the control unit. Throughout the remainder of 1937 and the first half of 1938, Edward continued to display signs of self-control. The problems continued to such an extent that the two establishments involved with the project were looking to either adapt the Queen Bee target drone control gear, or build special purpose equipment.

In the end it was found that a certain set of inputs on the No. 11 radio would cause excess radiation from the set which was flooding Edward's receiver with fake signals and causing the tank to drive itself. The solution was to use the old No. 9 set linked with a No. 11. This change was not a moment too soon. On 1 November 1938 a new demonstration was held. This time two Edwards performed flawlessly for ten minutes, being commended on the crisp highly responsive nature of their movements. The demonstration was brought to a halt when one of the Edwards threw a track.

For some reason at this high point the Edward project was wound up with a notification sent to the Air Ministry to stop work on 14 December 1938. Some discussions were held about fitting Edwards to A.12 Matilda Seniors to serve as gunnery targets, although there is no record of this being carried out.

THE SOLDIERLESS TANK

Winston Churchill viewing a Queen Bee target drone in 1941.

In France at some point in the late 1930s the French inventor Ernest Alphonse Derungs invented a way of controlling a craft remotely. The device was controlled by wire. These sets could be fitted to full-size vehicles, including aircraft, but the principal aim was for ships, the idea being that as a fleet approached a mined area the remotely-controlled ship could be sent ahead and used to find a safe passage which the rest of the force would then follow.

Three of these control units were built and fitted to tanks in 1940, before the German invasion, and a demonstration was held for both British and French officers at the Bourges arsenal. None of the dignitaries were impressed by the demonstration.

It was claimed by the French Colonel 'Martin-Prévell' (presumably a typo for Colonel Jacques Martin-Prével) that remote-controlled demolition vehicles were used successfully to destroy German armour hiding in a defile during the fighting at Sedan in 1940. The document which mentions this has a warning to accompany the claim, stating that MI10 (the British intelligence service concerned with technical developments) could find no evidence of the event happening. Colonel Martin-Prével crops up elsewhere – in Canada, where he seems to have convinced the Canadians of his expertise in armour design, and was involved with the failed Wolf 1 armoured-car project. It is known that a small prototype tracked demolition mine was recovered from France after the German invasion, and started the project which would result in the Goliath tracked mine.

Back in the UK on 3 February 1940 interest in Edward was renewed. There was some argument over the logistics of the project as the radio equipment was in one location and the tank in another. By the 20th Edward was run in a demonstration in front of the General Staff, but then went back into retirement.

A year later the deputy director of tank design wrote to the General Staff asking what was to become of Edward, as it was taking up space and, if it was not going to be renewed, he would like to scrap it. This letter brought the technology to the notice of Major General Pope, who immediately became interested, asking for the equipment to be fitted to a Valentine infantry tank with the aim of fitting it with flame, smoke or gas projection. The control equipment was to be mounted on an identical chassis, much like the earlier Soviet teletanks. Attempts were made to fit the Edward equipment to a Valentine, but the gearbox was the wrong type. It would, however, fit into a Matilda infantry tank. Installation began on 19 March 1941. In July the tank was re-named 'Black Prince'. With the new name, some interdepartmental problems were occurring with the radio-control equipment still being held by the Air Ministry. However, this did not stop the tank from running under wired control on 29 July. At about the same time discussions were being held about the idea of fitting the equipment to flame-thrower versions of the Churchill tank that were under development, but this came to naught.

At this point an officer in the Middle East theatre of operations contacted the War Office to ask if any work had been done on remotely-controlled tanks. The War Office replied that they had been doing joint work with the French, but as the western front had collapsed the work had halted. However, interest had recently been revived, and they asked if Middle East Command had any data on the subject it would like to share?

By 23 September trials with Black Prince had continued. The only major problem was that on extremely steep slopes the gears became erratic. In December work had finished on the controls for the tank, making it much simpler to use; it now employed a simple press-button system. A new demonstration, which was entirely successful, was held at the end of December. Following on from that demonstration, permission was sought for the production of sixty units, with four being given to each army tank brigade for the purposes of minefield detection, distraction and laying smoke screens.

Production did not follow, as the Ministry of Supply, which held control over all manufacture in Britain during the war, had a bottleneck in the production of radio equipment. By June 1942 the General Staff had written to the MoS asking that sixty units be constructed. By October a contract for the production of eighty-one radio sets had been placed; these would be fitted to Matilda Mk IV tanks. At this point the MoS asked how they should refer to the tanks. The response was 'Matilda (B.P)'. They predicted that the tanks would be ready in February 1943 and the Vulcan Foundry, the manufacturer of the Matilda, had agreed to become the principal contractor. Vulcan did raise concerns about their ability to complete the order without prejudicing their work on locomotives and also pointed out that they certainly could not store the converted Matilda tanks.

As Vulcan were busy with the aforementioned work they refused to build any tanks until they were producing the actual production model. This meant even more delay and all of the prototype re-design work would fall on the War Office. That, along with the shortage of firms with electro-pneumatic component production experience and the need to replace large parts of the steering with new designs, meant that there was significant investment of time and money for such a short run of vehicles. As the manufacture was extending further and further away it led to the entire project being wound up on 3 January 1943.

There were other experiments in the UK with unmanned tanks, although these were more along the lines of the German Goliath tracked mine, and did not use radio control.

In 1940 in Britain, Metropolitan Vickers had come up with a new idea, a small tracked vehicle, with each track driven by an electric motor, carrying 140lb of explosive. It was controlled by wires that spooled out from the back of the tank. Originally it was nicknamed Beetle but this was later changed to 'mobile land mine' or MLM.

After initial successful trials in August 1941, admittedly held under ideal conditions, an order for fifty was placed so that further trials could be carried out. These trials also required that the MLM be fitted with brakes and a safety mechanism. The trigger for the explosive was a tiller bar on the front of the device, and should the MLM bump into a tree it would detonate early.

On 22 September further experiments were carried out with a waterproofed version for use near shore. Floats were fitted and the MLM could be deployed as a floating mine, or the floats jettisoned and an attack

An early version of the Beetle undergoing testing. This picture actually shows the control apparatus, although one can only guess as the purpose of the wooden blocks.

The last version of the MLM, with the amphibious floats fitted.

run made along the bottom of the sea bed. Trials were successful and a landing craft was hit. Another variant was an airborne MLM, weighing in at 350lb that could be parachuted.

The MLM was running into some technical difficulties. It lacked the ability to pass through a fence, although this was later fixed, while 45-degree slopes would stop it, as would mud or an 18-inch vertical surface. Equally its speed of 5mph, initially, and, later, 12mph was insufficient to allow it to catch other tanks and 'torpedo' them. One observer reported that he watched a MLM try to catch a Universal carrier until the carrier simply drove out of range, dodging every attempt with ease. By 9 March 1942 the troop trials had been completed and the report on the MLM was quite critical.

On 2 April a hare-brained scheme for the employment of the MLM was suggested. A trip-wire was to be laid, and when an enemy tank drove over it, the trip wire would become entangled in the tracks after which the MLM would reel in the tripwire and thus track onto the target. It seems that this idea was not pursued.

There is a long political side to the MLM story as Metropolitan Vickers had enlisted the support of their local MP, Mr Ellis Smith. For some reason he was really impressed by the device and so began a campaign that lasted until May 1942 in which he was badgering for further orders despite the poor performance and trial reports. His campaign of letter writing included the Prime Minister, Deputy Prime Minister, along with various individuals representing government departments. It ended up with one of the people involved stating that Mr Smith's statement was a 'complete travesty of the true state of affairs'.

Finally, while on the subject, I need to mention the Ferret, another private venture, this time by John Allen and Sons of Oxford. It was about three times the length of the MLM, and about twice its width and height, but was a true land torpedo. With neither guidance nor remote control it would just run on a course until it hit a target. Its three-ton weight was powered by a 5hp engine with some extreme gearing which managed to move the projectile at 0.25mph. Due to its low speed, it was given heavy armour for its size. It was found to perform well, being able to smash through wire with considerable ease and, although not waterproofed, could operate in up to two feet of water.

However, its peculiar noise and slow speed meant that it was tactically limited, and it was felt that remotely-controlled devices were a better idea. Of course this tiny company could not have known about these devices.

Chapter 11

The Secret Life of the Infantry Tank

On hearing the term 'infantry tank' most people think of the concept as being a purely Second World War invention, one that first appeared with the A.11 Matilda and ended with the Churchill Mk VII. However, the infantry tank story starts much earlier than is commonly believed and is linked to the development of ideas from the decade before the A.11. The 1920s' machine was a very different form to the later ones. But the concept behind it led directly to the heavily armoured monsters the Germans learned to fear. At the other end of the story the infantry tank hung on for a few years after the war.

The first tank designated as an 'infantry tank' in British service seems to have been utterly unrelated to later developments. Shortly after the First World War Lieutenant Colonel Philip Johnson set up the Department for Tank Design. Johnson was the British version of Walter Christie or Ferdinand Porsche: all three designed what they wanted and not what was asked of them. Like Christie, Johnson thought that speed was the only concern in a tank. When he was asked to design a new tank for the British Army, one capable of leading an assault, Johnson's resulting design was called the Light Infantry Tank. It incorporated all the worst features from the disastrous Medium D, such as lack of a cannon, and the driver in a cupola on the roof of the tank, which created a blind spot about seven metres around the tank.

The Light Infantry Tank weighed only eight tons, but was powered by a 100hp engine. During tests it managed to get up to 30mph but, as it was not what the War Office had asked for, it was never ordered. From there the name infantry tank was not used again until 1925 when Giffard le Quesne Martel advanced, if not started, the idea of the infantry tank that would culminate with the Churchill.

Martel was a gifted engineer and built at least three prototype tanks in his own time to see if his ideas would be feasible. One, in 1930, was the very science-fiction-like four-track tank. It was a tank with four sets of tracks in series, an design never replicated on a tank, even with modern technology.

Johnson's Light Infantry tank (top) at the scrapyard after its life, and the Medium D (bottom) for comparison.

At the time Martel was in India, and the Indian Army had recently received Vickers light tanks which, while proving very satisfactory, were running into a problem. Like most things in tank design there is a trade off in the length of the tank: the longer the tracks the smoother the tank can drive across country. Against this the longer the track the harder it is to turn the tank. At the time most tanks used skid steering, and longer tracks increased the chances of throwing a track.

Martel asked himself a question: 'could you take a light tank, like the current Vickers machine, and increase its length by another five feet?' He worked out that if you had two sets of tank tracks, with the forward pair a steering set, like the wheels of a car, the tank could be longer. Such a set-up

Martel, and his four-track tank somewhere in India.

would have the benefits of length for cross-country work and yet keep the ease of steering.

With this in mind he constructed the prototype. All four tracks were powered, and the front tracks were steerable. Martel also used this opportunity to test a new type of track made from both rubber and steel.

The engine in the experiment was a 16hp Morris car engine supplied by Army HQ India but everything else was bought or constructed by Martel. The tank had a turning circle of just twelve feet which required, in the first build, twelve full turns of the steering wheel to give full lock. Martel modified the steering by using a gearing arrangement that reduced the requirement to six turns, which could be further reduced by altering the gearing. With this set-up Martel was able to drive the tank normally with one full turn being more than enough for road driving. For speed Martel only ran the vehicle at speeds of up to 12mph as there had been a mistake measuring the tracks and sprockets so that they did not fit properly, and would need to be re-made for a proper speed trial. The speed obtained had required almost no pressure on the accelerator to achieve, Martel noted. He also mentioned that it had much better cross-country ride performance than a Vickers Light.

The four track tank was 5 feet 5 inches high, but this was due entirely to the way the engine was mounted. For cheapness of construction it was placed high in the rear body. If expense was no problem then it could be lowered by 18 inches, giving a 3-feet-9-inches height.

Regarding expense, Martel's final report on the subject included a section about the costs and how, if they wished, the War Office could proceed by

Another picture of Martel putting his tank through its paces in India. You can see from this picture how the tank would negotiate rocks smoothly.

either leasing the tank and its tracks or buying the entire vehicle outright. Some idea of Martel's character can be obtained from the fact that he had angrily scribbled out that part of the report, and paid special attention to obliterating the figures of cost. However, this was all in the future, and first Martel needed to plant the seed that grows to the infantry tank that modern historians recognise.

In January 1925 Martel started work on what he called an 'infantry tank'. Later, during a presentation to the Imperial General Staff conference, Martel coined the title 'tankette'. With this name he hoped to describe the class as something between a tank and a transport for machine guns. Martel claimed this was at the 1927 conference, but in a report on the 1927 conference Martel's name is not listed as attending, and the Chief of the Imperial General Staff (CIGS) stated that the term 'tankette' had been abolished, and that armoured vehicles could be heavy, medium or light tanks, or carriers. With this in mind, it is likely that Martel meant 1926, and got his date wrong in his written account. Regardless, throughout the life of the one-man tankette idea it was sometimes called an infantry tank.

Martel's logic was that normal tanks were threatened with anti-tank guns. He saw that there were two answers to this: either make the tank so heavily armoured that it could resist the enemy's attentions, or make it lightly armoured and have a huge number of them attacking. His driving idea was dispersion. Much like the shift from blocks of infantry caused by the improvement in fire-arms in the 1800s, he saw the same happening with armour. In either case, Martel stressed that the tank should be cheap, which could be achieved by buying off-the-shelf components from the motor industry. He saw that there was a logical link to size, lightness, cheapness, and numbers, and started thinking along those lines. These infantry tanks, or 'tankettes', would be armed with a machine gun, and would provide armoured mobile firepower to lead and 'shoot in' an assault.

Martel also proposed that the tankette could be used as mechanised cavalry, and even drew up an organisation for the tankette cavalry company. Each squadron was to be four platoons strong, each with twenty men in four sections. Martel also provided them with a transport platoon of ten tankettes fitted with unarmoured box bodies capable of holding a half ton of stores. At the time, radios were not really viable in Martel's view for such small vehicles, so he suggested using runners to communicate; these would also be mounted in tankettes. Cavalry has traditionally been seen as a reconnaissance force, and it might have been from these seeds that the Tank Corps took Martel's idea and expanded it to become the light tank. Martel certainly blamed the Tank Corps for that in later years. He also warned, several times, against the 'improvement' of his ideas into something radically different from what the machine was designed for.

At the time the British Army was, as usual during times of peace, fighting the Treasury as well as being the policeman of the Empire. Martel knew that his ideas would not survive if they cost too much, and he made a cost analysis. The cost to buy a Renault FT was £1,500 (nearly £82,000 today) whereas his proposed one-man tank was about £400 (around £22,000 today). Martel also worked out the costs of a unit during peacetime, suggesting £30 (over £1,600 today) for annual running costs and a capital outlay of £80 (just

Proposed Tankette Company Organisation

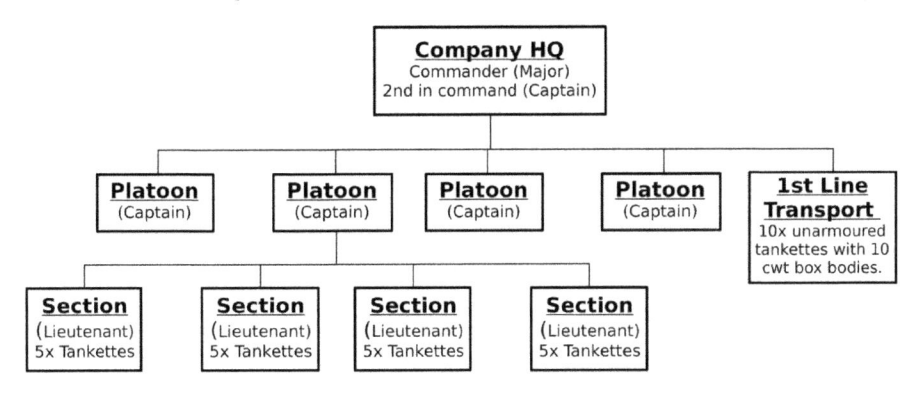

- **Company HQ** — Commander (Major), 2nd in command (Captain)
  - **Platoon** (Captain)
    - **Section** (Lieutenant) 5x Tankettes
  - **Platoon** (Captain)
    - **Section** (Lieutenant) 5x Tankettes
  - **Platoon** (Captain)
    - **Section** (Lieutenant) 5x Tankettes
  - **Platoon** (Captain)
    - **Section** (Lieutenant) 5x Tankettes
  - **1st Line Transport** — 10x unarmoured tankettes with 10 cwt box bodies.

under £4,400 today) per annum, based upon a five-year life, and a suspect claim that one set of tracks could last the entire life of the tankette. Martel argued that an entire 1,000-man battalion could be replaced at no extra cost with a 500-strong battalion of tankettes. He also proposed a handful of tankettes per infantry company; these would carry light automatic weapons.

A month later, in February 1925, he had the plans for his design laid out, and began to order parts. A 20hp engine manufactured by Maxwell was married to a Ford rear axle and Roadless Traction running gear.

Again the problems of an armoured vehicle's relative dimensions appeared. The tank was too high for its length, meaning that the centre of gravity was too high, while the back axle had all the torque running through it. The combination of these factors meant that the Tankette would have flipped over backwards. At first Martel considered having longer tracks than needed, but this added weight and cost. In the end he elected to have a stabiliser at the back of the vehicle. On the prototype this took the form of wheels from an old Federal lorry, which vehicle also provided all the steering gear.

By March Martel had amassed all the parts and set to work, finishing the first build by August. However, during the first trial, Martel found that

Martel's one man prototype scaling a hillside while several others observe. You can see instantly the importance of the stabiliser.

the gearing was wrong, as was the weight distribution, while the spring in the stabiliser was too light. By the end of August he had resolved these deficiencies. This was aptly proved by a coincidental meeting. In late August 1925, Martel took his machine out for a drive around the local area and, as he charged about, he passed an army officer out for a walk. The officer was none other than Captain Liddell Hart, who, surprised by this, filed a report with the *Daily Telegraph*, which was printed on 28 August:

> Surprise changed to awe when this twentieth century man-at-arms, mounted on his mechanical charger, climbed out of the road up an almost perpendicular bank at least four feet high, raced across a stretch of rough gorse country at a speed no runner could have approached and no horseman would have cared to attempt across such ground, turning abruptly in such a narrow circle that would have been the envy of a London taxi-driver. Next it headed for a small but steep hill, climbed it unfalteringly at a speed of 6-7mph, then threaded its way through a tree plantation which a horse or pack-mule could barely have traversed.

Several other demonstrations followed. Although the tankette was made of wood, painted grey, and armed with a wooden dummy machine gun, Martel had made sure to ballast his tank to represent those heavier items.

Martel applied for official permission to carry out trials using the tank in an amphibious nature. Since the inception of the tank the idea of landing them as part of an amphibious force had been considered. The size of the tanks had always caused problems during landing, those tanks available to the British in 1925 weighing at least ten tons. At first glance, Martel's tankette would appear to have been ideal.

However, the same official intransigence that had forced Martel to build the tankette himself forced him to arrange to carry out these trials without official sanction. Enlisting the help of the Navy, Martel transported his machine from his home to Gosport where the little tankette was loaded onto a Navy cutter which had been modified with a ramp at the rear. The launch set out, and then turned inshore near Gosport. The beach selected was mud and shingle. The cutter got as close as it could to the beach, then anchored itself, and swung its tail round to face the muddy incline of the beach before dropping the ramp. Although this seems like a long process, it only took moments.

An early one-man Tankette showing off its fording abilities during trials at Wool.

The tankette with Martel driving then began to disembark when disaster struck. The ramp's lip had not been smoothed in line with the hull and the tankette hit this rim and tipped forward, threatening to plunge one of Britain's brilliant military inventors into the sea, with two tons of tank on top of him. After stumbling, the tankette recovered itself and carried on down the ramp. The water was about one to two feet deep but this presented no trouble for the little tracked machine. Neither did the steep muddy banks which the tankette successfully climbed.

With the success of the demonstrations, the War Office decided to commission a pair of vehicles for testing. These were made from 8mm unarmoured steel. Another change was in the engine, which was switched to a Morris 16hp car engine. On Martel's advice, Morris Commercial Motors was selected as the company to build the tankettes and hence the suggested change of engine. The vehicle was designed so that the body could be unbolted from the chassis. This was done so that only one type of chassis need be constructed. Morris Ltd also shared Martel's vision that the chassis without a body could function as a tractor as well although this idea came to naught. Two bodies were also manufactured, one being a one-man machine, the other a two-man machine. From the description, the controls remained in the centre of the two-man machine so that either man could drive.

The construction of both Morris-Martel machines was finished in February 1926. In the final design, both machines were over three tons in weight when their projected weight had been closer to the original two tons. Testing at a disused mine near Birmingham confirmed that the weight caused problems and the tankettes were redesigned with a new chassis that cut out all the excess weight and the steel body was reduced to 6mm. It is likely that this was also the point that a redesigned stabiliser, with a single small wheel instead of two large ones was substituted. This diet got both tanks down to their projected two-ton weight, and the performance almost exactly matched the predicted figures.

Around this point, as the idea of the tankette began to gather traction, Martel was offered an award for the invention. Characteristically, he turned it down, stating that no officer had a moral claim for any work done when connected to military work. However, the question was pressed and, in the end, Martel accepted a payment to cover his expenses in construction of the prototype, and left the final decision on the subject open until a later date. The question remained open until September 1927, when Martel officially resigned from any claim to any financial award he might have in the invention of the tankette.

Further trials in March and April 1926 showed that, in some circumstances, the tank could become slightly overheated. Better ventilation was provided, along with an armour increase back up to 8mm. The tankettes also had problems with a lack of grip from the tracks, and a new track was designed and built, but was utterly ignored by the War Office. In addition, the tanks developed a steering wobble on hard roads but, although a solution was proposed, it, too, was not implemented.

This lack of progress was indicative of the situation that would leave the Morris-Martel design in limbo for a while before killing it off. From the start, Morris Ltd had been clear that they would not take up any of the technical development work for the machine but would simply build it to the specifications. Martel, as a serving engineer at the Experimental Bridging Establishment, was busy with his own work. The War Office's technical branch was not interested in any way in working on the problem. As the technical branch was also run by the Royal Artillery, they lacked the technical skills or knowledge to make decisions on tracked vehicles. This was a problem that Martel said plagued this period.

However, the War Office did order a further two machines in May 1926, and asked Morris Ltd to produce the vehicles as fast as possible since an immediate need for them was seen. Morris Ltd duly put its workers on

A pair of two-man Tankettes, one carrying a passenger, spoil the quiet of a small village near Salisbury.

Sunday working and overtime and in July informed the War Office that both their machines were ready for collection.

The War Office ignored the completed machines for three weeks, leaving them standing at Morris Ltd's works before collecting them. At the time this was considered really bad manners, and Morris Ltd were furious at the War Office, which further built on their reluctance to work on the tankettes.

The War Office then placed an order for eight new two-man tankettes for use in the mobile force. During September Martel found out that new tracks had not been ordered and the track problems had been ignored for months after he had designed the solutions. He was understandably livid and wrote a letter to the technical branch. It got results and the new, improved tracks were ordered from a different company who, not having any background on the subject, struggled to complete the order. However, they did finish the tracks but, true to form, these were left at the company's premises until, once again, Martel prompted the technical branch into action. The tracks were collected seven months late and sent to Farnborough, where they were further ignored.

In December 1926 Martel travelled to Morris Ltd to help with the order for the eight tankettes. He got around the lack of new-model tracks by getting Morris Ltd to weld projections onto the old tracks as an attempt to get some progress. As a stop-gap for the wobble, he had the chassis lengthened slightly.

The Crossley-Martel machine. As with the Martel Tankette, the wheels are at the rear of the vehicle.

The eight Morris-Martel machines were used on exercise in August and September 1927 and, although few in number, a much larger number was requested for the following year. It appears that the order was not placed.

There was another Martel one-man tankette, the Crossley-Martel, which outwardly looked very similar to the Morris-Martel machine, although with the engine at the back and with much smaller tracks. The tracks themselves were Kregresse rubber tracks; Martel started work on fitting these to the one-man tank in January 1926. Martel passed his plans to Crossley Motors, who acted slowly and did not start construction until September. The machine was delivered in May 1927 and performed in much the same way as the Morris-Martel, only that it had cured the steering wobble and could reach 30mph. Martel considered this one of the best tankettes of the time. Despite Crossley Motors taking such a long time to build it, they had delivered it with holes in the bodywork. The Crossley-Martel was run for four months, during which it covered 1,000 miles. During this time the dust kicked up by the tracks entered the holes in the bodywork and smothered the engine. The testing department criticised the engine and its performance quite heavily, pointing out that they had had to change the engine at least once in the four months. Martel responded by pointing out that, if they had bothered to close up the holes caused by the manufacturing defects, this would not have been a problem. Martel pointed out some flaws in the design, such as the body being too high and trouble with the suspension, but overall he was satisfied with the design.

A number of the earlier one- and two-man Morris-Martel machines may be seen in the footage of the 1926 Dominion Premiers' demonstration at Camberley where they were driving alongside the Carden-Loyd one-man tankettes, of which eight were ordered at the same time as the eight Morris-Martels. However, with the demise of the Morris venture into the 'infantry tank' the baton passed firmly to Carden-Loyd.

In 1925 John Carden and Vivian Loyd started work on the same idea. However, their first machine was more a tracked motorcycle, with the crewman sitting astride the engine and two tracks on either side. It was rather low, the driver's head being just three feet off the ground. During its trials in March it failed on many aspects but, almost immediately, the Carden-Loyd machine was re-built with the engine at the back and the driver sitting at the front. Steering was provided by a simple bicycle handlebar which, when tilted one way, would apply the brake on that side although, at higher speeds, it promised no end of trouble.

Both machines lacked any form of armour. The idea was that speed and concealability would make up for the lack of armour plate, a notion that was

The Carden-Loyd machine after its rebuild.

quickly dropped, as even 8mm of armour would provide some protection from artillery fire.

The Carden-Loyd one-man tankette may also be seen in footage of the Camberley Dominion Premiers' demonstration of 1926. They appear in a variety of forms, some as wheel-cum-track machines. One machine in the footage is missing the gun shield that made up the turret affair around the Lewis gun. This was because, during the demonstration where both vehicles appeared together, one of the Morris-Martel machines collided with the Carden-Loyd, the turret of which was knocked badly, blocking the view of the driver who simply shoved it aside and off his vehicle and carried on with the show.

At the end of 1926, at the same time that the order for the eight two-man Morris-Martel machines was placed, eight Carden-Loyd machines were also ordered. These, too, would be two-man machines as, by this stage, thinking in the War Office was opposed to one-man tanks because of the difficulties arising from a single man driving and fighting, and due to the 'moral' superiority. From this order of eight machines, the Carden-Loyd would grow eventually into the Universal carrier.

In 1933 Martel boiled the basic idea of the one-man tank down as far as it could go. Indeed Martel suggested that his newest idea should be thought of not as a tank, but as infantry equipment, like a suit of armour.

Martel's third home-built armoured vehicle, the Mechanical Coffin. During battle the soldier could lie flat inside, and the gun-shield at the front would slide flat.

His paper covered much the same ground as his earlier work, talking of the need for dispersion and concealment, beginning an interesting tactical review of the First World War, the problems discovered during the fighting, and the main causes of casualties amongst the infantry. Martel's paper was entitled 'A Light Automatic Carrier' and was written to prove that the main problems from the First World War could be defeated by the use of his newest machine. To gain some support and raise interest, on one of the plans submitted with the paper Martel scribbled a question. It read simply:

What is this?
a. *A good joke?*
b. *A bad joke?*
c. *A devious engine of war?*
d. *A mechanical coffin?*

Somewhat unsurprisingly, the last option became the Light Automatic Carrier's new nickname.

The 'mechanical coffin' was an armoured bathtub driven by a 4hp motor which gave the contraption a speed of about 20mph. The body was bulletproof through 45 degrees either side. Heightwise it was about 1-foot-8-inches tall, and about 7-feet long. Driven by two very simple tracks on

Martel stands at attention beside his newly built Mechanical Coffin in a series of pictures that demonstrate its capacity. This picture is to demonstrate the low height of the vehicle.

In this picture the Mechanical Coffin has been fitted with its wheels for use on long distance marches away from combat.

These two images show the extremely basic construction of the A.11. The top image is the very first prototype of the A.11.

either side of the body, for longer road marches it could be fitted with a tricycle arrangement of wheels, the rear two being driven by the motor and the forewheel steered by a sort of tiller. The wheels were detachable from the frame, and so it was not a true wheel-cum-track machine.

As the soldier got closer to the enemy position he was to attack, the wheels would be removed and the mechanical coffin would continue on its tracks; within about 800 yards the driver would assume a prone position and pull a roof cover over for protection. When he was in position close to the enemy line he would raise the cover to form an armoured loophole through which he could put his light machine gun to deliver sustained close-range automatic fire into the enemy lines. These types of vehicles were also known as 'infighters', and one of the early Carden-Loyd two-man tankettes was later uparmoured and named the same, with the same role in mind. It seems that this concept was soon dropped by the army.

On 4 October 1933 Martel received the official reply. The Army saw no chance of the little mechanical coffin being used or taken up. The letter was signed by one of the leading thinkers in British tanks at the time, Vyvyan Pope, who asked Martel to keep him abreast of developments if he decided to go ahead with the idea.

Martel, of course, did decide to build the Mechanical Coffin. He noted that it was done mostly to teach his son about engineering, and claims it was mostly constructed by his son.

In November 1934, much to Martel's horror, the *Daily Telegraph* got hold of the story and ran a piece on the idea of the mechanical coffin and the concept of the infighter, quoting sources saying that a larger two-man version was under consideration and blaming the higher echelons of the War Office for the loss of this unconventional idea.

Martel, not wishing to prejudice his invention, immediately wrote to the War Office. He received a reassuring letter that mentioned that there was no need to worry and that the CIGS had penned the following memo:

> Martel's ideas and inventions, though some of them are a bit fantastic, are always worth considering with a view to further development. Now that we are after the armoured M.G. Carrier and may before long be after an armoured light auto carrier we should keep his idea in mind.

Now in the story of the infantry tank we come to more familiar territory, the A.11 Matilda. This first came into life in 1935, raised from an idea of Percy

Hobart. It is interesting to note that Vyvyan Pope was deployed at about the same time with Percy Hobart to Egypt, so they moved in the same circles and it is possible that Pope mentioned Martel's ideas to Hobart, if he had not already seen them himself.

However, more than that links the A.11 to the earlier one-man designs, as well as the title 'infantry tank'. A key point of the Matilda was the fact that it had to be cheap, using off-the-shelf components from the motor industry. It was also designed to be a simple armoured machine-gun carrier to support infantry assaults. The idea seems to have been, according to David Fletcher, to amass a large number of these tanks and overwhelm the defenders. In fact the only difference between Martel's and Hobart's ideas was the armour thickness.

From the A.11 Matilda may be traced a direct line of development through the Second World War to the Churchill series of infantry tanks before, the conventional thinking goes, the idea was abandoned. However, it appears that the concept of the infantry tank had one last card to play.

On 14 May 1948 a General Staff specification was issued for a new infantry tank, about which only fragmentary letters survive in the National Archives. It was referred to in the letters as the 'WB1'. Weighing in at seventy tons and with a speed of 20mph, it was only required to have a power-to-weight ratio of 0.75hp per ton. Those figures seem rather unusual, but the reason for that was the tank's armour. It was to have a basis of 400mm through the frontal 60-degree arc with the roof proof against 5.5-inch artillery shells detonated within two feet of the vehicle. The tank was also be capable of resisting a 25lb landmine.

Weaponry was to be a gun with eighty rounds, with the smoke and HE capabilities to be the same as the contemporary 77mm gun. The specifications also called for armour penetration performance of 125mm against plate sloped to 30 degrees at 2,000 yards range, which again was the performance of the 77mm gun. This was probably the General Staff's way of saying that they wanted the 77mm gun fitted, which was an odd choice, as by then they were already looking at 105mm and even 120mm guns, as even the 20-pounder and 90mm guns of the United States were seen as lacking. It might be that they wanted raw rate of fire, which was something they were unlikely to get as the design was considered to be rather cramped due to the heavy use of sloping armour.

Other requirements included full climate control and protection against nuclear, biological and chemical weapons, and infra-red driving equipment.

A few months later, on 22 June, A.E. Masters, Chief Engineer of the Fighting Vehicles Development Establishment, replied to the General Staff specifications. Simply put, he was having trouble fitting all the requirements into the tank. By his maths, the best the frontal armour could be was 350mm and the side 100mm. The engine size would be limited to something akin to the Centurion's engine, which would limit the speed to just 17mph. Finally, to get a sufficient amount of travel in the suspension, the crew compartment had to be smaller than normal, leading to the cramped interior. After this no other records for the WB1 or indeed any other infantry tank seem to exist. The concept of the infantry tank lasted a quarter of a century, and provided some of the finest armoured vehicles on the Allied side in the Second World War, until the role was finally taken over by the Universal or Main Battle Tank.

Chapter 12

The Tanks without a War

In the previous chapter I may have given the impression that Giffard Martel was somewhat eccentric. This is not necessarily the case as, for example, Martel played a key part in development of armoured bridge-layers at the Experimental Bridging Establishment. Looking at some of his designs it is instantly recognisable, even today, that he was on the right track. Martel also worked hard to bring the War Office back from some of their peculiar logic and thinking in regards to tank classification.

In May 1947 a civil servant was tasked with trying to work out what the War Office's tank policy was in 1939. With the usual dutifulness of these types of summaries, the civil servant ploughed into the relevant documents and tried to write a narrative. What he found, and all of what he submitted, was several pages of argument over whether a tank was classified as a 'heavy cruiser' or a 'cruiser'; indeed he did not seem to be able to find anything approaching a policy as we would recognise it today. To muddy the waters even further, the 'heavy cruiser' was also, on occasion, called the 'battlecruiser', and there was also some talk of a 'light cruiser', although the latter never seemed to get tied to a class. It was suggested, briefly, that the A.17 Tetrarch (formally named the 'Purdah') was a candidate, which gives a possible outline of the capabilities of the 'light cruiser'. It also does not help that 'light tank' is sometimes applied to tanks described as 'cruisers'. So what did these classes actually mean?

After reading the best efforts of the unknown civil servant several times, the difference appears to be almost non-existent. The best I can do is the wafer-thin distinction that cruisers are for skirmishing with the enemy, and heavy cruisers are for when the skirmishing ends and the enemy has to be fought in a stand-up battle. The main difference that turns a cruiser into a heavy cruiser seems to be the addition of a sub-turret with a machine gun. There did not seem to be any extra armour, as one might expect, although the narrative also included plans to increase the armour on the front of all cruisers from 30mm to 40mm basis, while leaving the sides at their existing 30mm basis.

This A.10 cruiser tank was captured by the Germans in Greece. The front hull machine gun that caused problems for the classification by the War Office has been removed. It would normally be located above the damaged head light.

Part of the argument was around the A.10 tank, as that had a hull-mounted machine gun and thus was neither a heavy nor a regular cruiser. The back and forth in the documents also admits that a normal cruiser could do the job of a heavy cruiser and vice versa. Luckily, in some ways, the Second World War broke out four months later and prevented the thinking of the War Office from forming another sub-class of cruiser tank and making future tank historians' lives even more difficult.

The nearest to a policy I can find is from a meeting held on 16 May 1938. The minutes include a list of numbers of tanks to be built, a total of 585 of all classes of cruisers, of which 268 would be normal cruisers; all of those were to be A.13s. The remaining 317 would be heavies with A.9s and A.10s making up 200 of this number in an equal split. The remaining 117 were to be A.16s, which we will consider towards the end of this chapter.

This entire situation started in 1928 where the seeds of the curious thinking that prevailed on the outbreak of the Second World War were founded. At the time the British were using the Vickers Medium Mk II, a tank whose creation is shrouded in mystery (for a possible hint, see the earlier chapter about tractor tanks) and that seemingly came out of nowhere at just the right time to save the British tank units and, incidentally, relieve the War Office of a large troublesome fund of money that would be reclaimed by the Treasury if not spent on tanks in that financial year. The Medium Mk II was given to the experimental mechanised force to use in trials, where it was quickly found that it would be unsuitable for use in the same way as cavalry, due to its large size and slow speed. During the exercises in 1928 Brigadier R.J. Collins was commanding the tank force, while his opponent, commanding a traditional infantry force, was Colonel A.P. Wavell. Both came to the conclusion that the most important factor in the tank was mobility. This was because they realised that the infantry had sufficient weapons in the form of field guns and dedicated anti-tank guns to wreck any attacking armoured force, but only if those guns were allowed to be massed at one point. Equally, when moving about, the infantry was often described as conducting 'undignified scrambles, by dark if possible' from one terrain feature to another that provided defence against armoured attack. The idea was to catch the infantry in the middle of these moves and wipe them out when they had not the opportunity to set up their anti-tank weapons. Or, if the enemy had set up, then the tanks could use their mobility to be elsewhere, away from the concentration of opposing anti-tank weapons.

This thinking shines through in January 1929 when these two officers gave a presentation to the General Staff conference, in which they suggested that the ideal tank would be one that focused on mobility first, firepower second and protection third; the ratio of importance was suggested at 3-2-1. Another officer involved also suggested that the ideal for a tank would be a light tank, but armed with the gun of a medium. Considering the cruiser tank the British went to war with, the A.13, this ratio may be seen plainly: the excellent 2-pounder mounted on a very mobile chassis, but with protection limited to stopping small-arms fire.

Finally, Colonel Wavell described the situation with an analogy, comparing the tank force to that of a Royal Navy fleet: 'the battle fleet, which is protected by a screen of destroyers (light tanks), against submarine attack (concealed anti-tank guns).' The origin of the designation 'cruiser' is plain to see.

It is a shame that this thinking came about at the time the British Army had just received its newest tank, the A.6E3, or the 16-tonner. Although not heavily armoured, having just 14mm, it did carry a good 3-pounder gun, and up to five .303 Vickers machine guns, although the latter arrangement was part of a trial to see if twin or single machine guns in the sub-turrets were more practicable. It was quickly realised that the single machine gun worked

The A.6 with twin Vickers guns in its sub-turrets.

better, and so this was implemented. More importantly, the A.6E3 was a tank with room for development. At the same 1929 conference that started the demise of the medium tank, the Director of Mechanisation, Major General S.C. Peck, explained that the development of a diesel engine had made great strides in the previous year, and that soon one would be fitted to the A.6 medium tanks. However, it appears that this did not actually happen, despite the British establishment being very aware of all the benefits of the diesel engine, including the fuel being cheaper to produce by a farthing per gallon.

As well as the A.6, which had arrived in 1928, there two other tanks, both manufactured at the same time, under the designation A.7. Aimed at being about 10 tons, they spent most of their time closer to the weight of the A.6 and, like the A.6, carried a 3-pounder gun. These tanks were the A.7E1 and A.7E2, which were used for assorted trials, although not delivered until 1931. Most of the developments on the A.6E3 were suspension related, with the A.6E3 said to have outrun several other vehicles in a cross-country demonstration in October 1930.

With both the A.6 and A.7 in the field in the early 1930s they were used as development platforms and slowly altered with different or new suspension systems being introduced. It was not until 1934 that the pace of development began to pick up. In the case of the A.7, work and research began looking at combining the ideas of the previous two models into an improved version, the A.7E3.

This is the A.7E1. Later models may be distinguished by the suspension brackets along the lower part of the side skirts and the round front hatch. On the A.7E3 the turret had a mantle and a 2-pounder gun.

Through the first half of 1934, and presumably the latter half of 1933, the General Staff requirements for the A.7E3 were being tweaked and finalised. In part, these were driven by the twin questions: 'What does the War Office want?' and 'What is the War Office likely to get?'

The earliest surviving documents start in January 1934 when a committee recommended that the engines be water-cooled as air-cooled engines had not been a success. Two weeks later engines were reviewed again, with the recommendation for using twin commercial type engines. Associated Equipment Company (AEC) was asked to run an investigation into the problem with a contract, number V/2604, being placed on 21 February 1934. The investigation was complete by June, in which AEC recorded, unsurprisingly, that twin AEC six cylinder 7.7L compression ignition (called 'CI' engines, or diesel) omnibus engines be used. These fed into twin Wilson gearboxes with their outputs coupled. Apart from a note about the A.7E3 requiring sufficient financial backing, nothing else seems to have happened in 1934.

In 1935 a series of trials was scheduled to determine which suspension to use on a new tank design. These were between a modified A.7E2, the A.6E3 and a Vickers Medium Mk III, registration T870. The aim was to test suspensions; the A.7E2 was fitted with Luvax suspension, while the A.6E3 was fitted with a brand new Horstman suspension. The trials were carried out on 11 April 1935. The A.7E2 was ballasted up with an extra ton of weight, and baulks of timber were laid out on a road and the tanks run over it. The A.7E2 won easily, but the observers from Vickers were not convinced that their suspension on the A.6E3 had worked as they thought and claimed that they could do better. They took the tank away and on the 30th returned with the modified tank. The trial was re-run with both the A.6E3 and the A.7E2 having equal results. So, as a tie break, a ten-mile run over rough pasture was conducted. In this A.6E3 was judged to have won, achieving speeds up to 25mph. Meanwhile the A.7E2, with an old, worn-out engine could not achieve its speed of 15mph. Both suspensions could be firmed up to provide a stable gunnery platform, which could be done from the driver's position while buttoned down. Thus a gunnery comparison was scheduled as soon as both tanks had been repaired. The Luvax suspension was approved for the A.7E3, while the Vickers Horstman suspension was approved for the A.8 medium.

The A.8 was a proposal from Vickers, submitted in January 1933. After review, a General Staff requirement for the tank was issued. Armoured to 14mm and with a speed of 25mph, this was a 17.5-ton tank. By the performance numbers on the specification, it seems to have been very close to an evolved A.6 or A.7. There were two differences from the previous tanks. First, the firepower was to be the usual 3-pounder and co-axial .303 machine gun, but, in the hull, only one sub-turret was to be fitted, armed with either a .303- or a .5-inch machine gun. The engines selected were a pair of Rolls Royce Phantom II petrol engines which were to be linked. This latter choice caused some considerable anguish in the War Office and resulted in two senior officers proceeding 'to discuss this thorny question verbally'. The argument was because the Rolls Royce engines were being used by the Royal Air Force and, with only a limited number produced each year, putting them in tanks meant an insecure supply as the Air Ministry had priority. In the end it was agreed that these engines could be used only for experimental tanks, and not for production tanks. With this proviso in place, authorisation was given to go ahead. A mock-up was ready for viewing at a meeting about the A.8E1 on 9 October 1933. At the meeting the following changes were requested: the driver's position had been designed as totally closed down at all times, but it was requested that the driver be able to drive unbuttoned; skirting plates were also to be included. What followed was several months of financial wrangling between the War Office and Vickers about where the money was coming from, one offshoot of that being the decision to mount the A.7 turret design on the A.8.

THE TANKS WITHOUT A WAR

Then there seems to have been a further falling out about finances between the government and Vickers, with the government wanting the Vickers-Horstman suspension to be fitted free of charge, something Vickers refused to do. It may be that this disagreement was what killed off the A.8 project, as the project was cancelled shortly afterwards.

A curious worry cropped up on the A.7 project. A single memo mentions that there were concerns that frequencies of '70 and under' were likely to cause sickness in personnel. This memo does not record what sickness, or what they were measuring the frequencies in but does mention that they had been unable to confirm the phenomenon.

A picture of the interior of a Valentine tank turret. The gunner is on the left, as is the shoulder stock of the 2-pounder mount. With this he could move the gun up and down with his shoulder aiming the gun like a giant rifle.

The A.7E3 was delivered for gunnery trials on 10 April 1937. Previously it had been at Farnborough for automotive trials from about November 1936. It was delivered with faults in the co-axial machine-gun gearing, which prevented firing, and with at least one suspension bogie missing. By the 21st the engine had seized, along with several bogies, bringing the trials to an end. Despite this, the A.7E3 seemed a much better machine than the earlier models, having a 2-pounder gun, as well as being able to mount the Vickers 3-inch howitzer. It also carried two machine guns, one mounted co-axially, the other in the hull with a 100-degree arc. It was able to achieve a speed of 25mph on a road and 18mph across country, could maintain a speed of 10mph on a slope, cross an 8-foot trench, and surmount an obstacle of 2.5-feet in height. Importantly, it also had a diesel engine. Armour-wise, it retained the 14mm armour basis.

The A.7E3 was soon to be the subject of an attempt at modifications. First was the turret, which received some experimental modifications, apparently centred around the gun-elevation gear. Famously, the British tanks with a 2-pounder had a shoulder-shoved gun, with the weapon resting on the shoulder of a standing gunner, who used his legs to stabilise it as the tank moved about. Like its contemporaries, the A.7E3 was fitted with a No. 2 free mounting. However, in November 1936, there was a proposal to fit the No. 1 geared mounting, taken from the A.9 tank. At roughly the same time there was an investigation running to see if the A.7E3 could be fitted with the Liberty engine, an investigation that concluded that it could with only a minor modification of the roof over the engine bay. Another hypothetical modification was the suggestion to fit Horstman-type suspension.

So there you have the state of affairs when two officers we have encountered before reappear. In 1936 General Wavell and Lieutenant General Martel were part of a military mission to Russia to view manoeuvres near Minsk. The mission took an overland route and passed through Berlin where they met Colonel Frederick Hotblack, the British military attaché in Hitler's Third Reich. Over dinner, Hotblack recounted a story he had just experienced about German attempts at re-armament and improving their army.

The Germans kept on receiving reports of British inefficiency which confused Hitler greatly because, despite the inefficiency, the British armed forces carried on succeeding. Obviously, he wanted to find out how the British achieved this and apply it to the German army to make it more efficient. To this end, Hitler ordered an enquiry into the subject. After its deliberations, the German enquiry came to the conclusion that the British sense of humour was responsible. Somewhat predictably Hitler decreed that

THE TANKS WITHOUT A WAR

So Offensichtlich
Der junge und geschwätzige: "Wie kommt denn das Loch da rein?"
Dem alles egal ist: "War ne Maus."

Erklärung: Selbstverständlich war das keine Maus!

the Germans should try to instill a British sense of humour in the German army. However, they did it in a very German way. First they tried to teach jokes by numbers, a plan that failed miserably.

Undeterred they tried a new approach. The idea was to let the soldiers soak up the humour naturally. They took a number of Bruce Bairnsfather's cartoons (creator of the 'if you know of a better 'ole' cartoon) and translated the jokes directly into German. Every week a new poster would be displayed in all the barracks across Germany. Colonel Hotblack asked if he might view the first trial carried out by the Germans, to which the Germans happily agreed.

The first cartoon selected to improve the German soldier had a picture of two soldiers standing next to a huge hole in a brick wall made by a very large artillery shell. One soldier asks the other, 'What made the hole?' to which he gets the sarcastic reply 'A mouse'.

When Colonel Hotblack arrived, he found the German translation of the cartoon in poster form but, at the bottom, the Germans had had to add another line, to explain the joke. In this case the German addition read 'Of course the hole was not really made by a mouse at all!'

With a straight face Colonel Hotblack stood aside and the first unit of Germans was marched in, turned to face the poster, and ordered to read the writing so that they might absorb the British humour. After they had dutifully done so, they were marched out. Not one of them had so much as smiled. Unsurprisingly this programme of improvements was immediately dropped.

After this brief interlude the military observers continued to the Minsk exercises where they spent four days watching about 1,200 Soviet tanks in action. This was a fraction of the total Soviet Union's tank force of the time which was over 13,000. Just eight years earlier, during a debate on how tanks were used, and how to defend against them, a British staff officer was on record as saying:

> infantry are set upon by tanks and other horrible devices until the poor infantry officer has very little time to think about carrying out his job. It is important to train in all these things, but we are getting a wrong sense of proportion as to what we are to expect in a war. To produce sufficient armoured vehicles to attack us in anything like the way we attack our own infantry in peacetime, the enemy will require 4,000 at least. I don't know of an army which has any intention of producing anything like this number of armoured vehicles. I cannot

believe that our infantry will ever be attacked in anything like the way we attack our infantry in peace training.

Then, after this demonstration at Minsk, the military mission travelled on to Moscow. From this hub they travelled around the region, visiting several military bases and manufacturing complexes. Martel and Wavell both came to different conclusions from this demonstration of the Soviet tank force. Wavell, one presumes, took the demonstration of speed and Christie suspension to heart and maybe thought back to his part in the 1929 conference. Martel, however, had other ideas forming on the way home.

This train of thought was briefly interrupted when leaving Minsk and about to cross the Russian border into Poland. At the time the Soviet Union had strict currency controls in place, which prevented the removal of roubles from the country. At the border an official appeared and asked the travellers if they were carrying any money. The British officers admitted that they were, and also said that they realised they would have to surrender it. The Russian official helpfully pointed out that this sort of eventuality had been foreseen and there was a list of societies that a traveller could join, and to which they could donate their monies. After reading the list the British officers all started laughing and instantly subscribed to the 'Society for the assistance of Individuals in Russia who were being persecuted by the communists'. The Russian officials found this quite hilarious as well.

Upon their return it is likely that Wavell began to agitate for the Christie suspension, and cruiser tanks, or at least someone who read his reports did, and the rest they say is history. Wavell would put his theories of armoured warfare to good use against the Italians in the North African desert.

As we have seen, Martel, now appointed to the Master General of the Ordnance department, was quite happy to be designing and building his own tanks and so started a new project, this time to design a full-sized medium tank. In his endeavours, he set up a small cabal of tank officers, including Liddell Hart. The medium tank Martel designed seems to have gained the nickname 'Monster'. For a year the group worked its influence but the Master General of the Ordnance, Lieutenant General Sir Hugh Elles, and Major General Alexander Elliott Davidson, the Director of Mechanisation, were opposed to the tank. By June 1937 these officers were considering tanks for the 1938 financial year. Although the A.7 was still about and technically a medium, it in no way fulfilled the General Staff requirements for a medium tank. The A.6 was closer to meeting the requirements, although falling some way short, which supports the claim that the A.6 was a tank ahead of its time.

On 9 June, Davidson forwarded two blueprints for consideration. One was a curiosity of which we have just a description. Based on the hull of an A.12 Matilda, how it differed from a normal infantry tank, or even what the turret looked like, we do not know. The second set of plans were the ones on which Martel had been working previously, and would in time become the A.14E1. A board met in committee on the 15th to review the situation and decide upon a course of action. After the current designs, A.6 and A.7, were reviewed, the board agreed that, if a Wilson-style steering was used, then a mere 15hp per ton would be sufficient to meet the General Staff requirements.

From this starting point the board reverse-engineered the maximum upper limit for the weight of the tank by comparing it to available engines and their horsepower. The four engines considered were the Liberty, with 400hp giving a tank of 24 tons, and the Meadows V12 with 430hp, giving a tank weight of 26.5 tons. Then came an interesting consideration, the Napier Lion engine, already fitted to the Supermarine S.4 and S.5 racing seaplanes, which would, eventually, lead to the Spitfire. The engine was also fitted to the British powerboat companies Type 2 high-speed launch, a craft that would later be used by the RAF's search and rescue units during the Second World War. The Lion produced the same 430hp as the Meadows V.12.

The engine finally selected was the Thornycroft RY12, which had an output listed at 575hp. This gave the tank weight of 32.5 tons. The 575hp output is curious since the original engine only produced 548hp but, by the end of April, a set of Simms dual ignition had been fitted which pumped its power output up to 607hp. After selection for the medium tank, the power requirements were reviewed and the engine derated by carburettor adjustment. After this modification, a test programme was run with the engine doing eighty-five hours at differing speeds and loads without a single problem. Furthermore, a second of these engines, linked to a specially-designed Borg and Beck clutch, was able to complete a test programme of 500 hours running when fitted to the A.6E3.

The board then turned its attention to the two blueprints on offer. The A.12-based one was rejected for unspecified reasons, but the second was much better liked, although it did have its flaws. In the eyes of the board the main difficulty was that it only had a single sub-turret on the left side. The board noted that if Martel's original design could be altered to carry two sub-turrets, the Martel design would be viewed favourably.

THE TANKS WITHOUT A WAR

The board's requirements for a medium tank are worth studying. The requirements were called '1938 class medium tank' and, in most respects, match those of the A.14E1 as eventually produced. However, there was a noticeable difference at first glance. The A.14 had a six-man crew, but the requirements had a seven-man crew, the spare man being located in the turret. Presumably, he was there to help take care of the plethora of weaponry crammed into the turret, which included a high-angle smoke mortar, a dedicated .303 anti-aircraft machine gun (which may also have had its own sub-turret at the rear of the tank; differing sources state different things) and, most intriguingly of all, the main gun was listed as a 2-pounder

A captured Czech ZV vz. 37 machine gun in German service in 1941. The main visual differences between the Besa and the ZB37 were the stock being replaced by a pistol grip, and no ribbing on the barrel. (Source: Bundesarchiv)

with an 'automatic feed'. There was also the requirement that a howitzer could be fitted if need be.

Some more modern sources indicate that all the machine guns on the tank were to be air-cooled, and the Czech ZB machine gun (later the Besa machine gun) was discussed as a possible candidate. These were located with two twin-mountings in each sub-turret and a single machine gun mounted co-axially to the main gun. Another difference was that the requirement was for 25 tons in weight. When the A.14 was produced, it had a weight of 29 tons, and the board was hoping to fit in an extra man, and automatic feed for the gun, as well as fifty more rounds and the same difference in number of miles range, all under the same armour protection. This was a wildly optimistic weight. The armour on the tank was given as 30mm basis, 20mm protecting the engine and everywhere else as 25mm.

On 17 June another meeting was held. As well as the officers present before, Percy Hobart and Martel were also there. This meeting's goal was to determine what tank would be built immediately. As well as the A.14, the A.7, A.9 and A.10 were all discussed. Hobart led a determined case for the idea of the sub-turret to be retained, stating that it was the only fitting that gave sufficient arcs of fire and, to avoid a blind side, two turrets were needed. Hobart, however, fared less well in his second point of contention. He was opposed to producing the A.9 as a stop-gap, which became the board's first decision. While the A.9 was being produced, in the medium term two of the new mediums would be produced. At this point the tank received its official designation of A.14. The long-term goal, however, was not production of the A.14; the tank was to be redesigned to give experience in the class so that a new medium tank could be designed meeting the requirements issued by the General Staff. The tank to meet the requirements would be numbered A.15. The designation A.15 was later re-issued for the A.15 Crusader. The medium tank to follow on from the A.14 had nothing to do with Crusader. This view was re-affirmed, when, in late February 1938, the Director of Mechanisation described the role of the A.14 as:

> The A.14 is a prototype of a medium tank which it is proposed to develop as rapidly as possible, so that if a heavy and fast medium tank of this nature is needed in the future, we shall be ready.

Some branches in the Mechanisation Board were opposed to the 1938 class specifications on several grounds, such as the range of the weaponry, which 'clashed badly', the complicated armour layout, and the four-man turret which would increase the width of the tank. It was this last point that caused the 1938 class to fail. After several discussions and changes of mind over the rail-loading gauge (even at one point considering using the continental loading gauge) the tank was dropped due to its width.

Before that, on 24 June, official confirmation that the A.14 was to be progressed was issued. For once, the A.14 was issued a name, albeit a slightly dismissive one. It may also have just been an internal description from Davidson, who referred to it as 'Modified Monster'.

At the very end of June, the subject of engines was revisited. As well as the ones mentioned before, the Paxman Ricardo V12 and Rolls Royce Kestrel were considered, as well as two foreign engines, listed only as the 'Isotta Fraschini' and the 'Lorraine'. The latter two were dismissed due to difficulties in obtaining large numbers, and on the grounds of not having a secure supply under the government's control. There was also some concern that minor variations were being constantly worked into these two engines during production, which could lead to non-standard parts. In the end the meeting confirmed the previous decision.

The meeting also considered the suspension. It was decided to use Vickers-Horstman type suspension as that would lead to development work on the type. The meeting saw no point in having two companies (Nuffield Mechanisation Ltd was working on Christie-type suspension) work on the same suspension design and would rather develop two separate designs so that, should one prove clearly superior, it could be used as the standard.

Now that a plan of action had been selected the War Office started trying to fit the modifications into the 'Monster'. From the start, this monster put

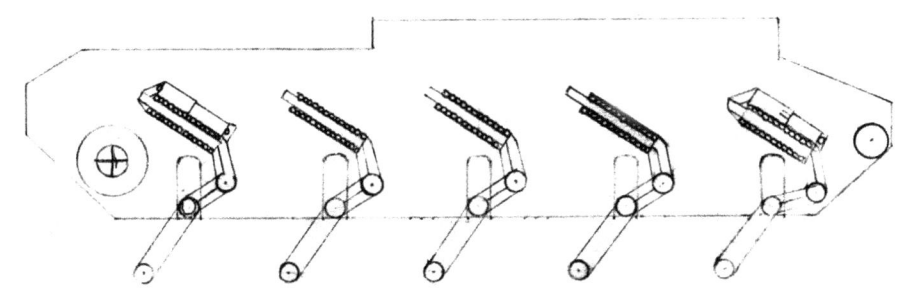

A set of suspension plans for the A.15, showing only the hull shape. The document from which this is taken does not record if this is the Crusader or the A.15; if the latter, it is the only clue we have to how the A.15 would look.

up a fight. The General Staff requirement was for a tank of 25 tons, but with the redesign to incorporate the twin sub-turrets, the projected weight climbed rapidly to 28 tons. Why, one would, ask was this a problem, since the earlier meeting had worked out that the Thornycroft RY12 could move a tank of over thirty tons? At the meeting on the 17th, and later, the complaint was that design trends in British tanks were to fit underpowered engines, and so the board wanted to keep plenty of power in reserve which, in turn, would allow further development of the chassis.

One of the steps suggested to cut the weight of the tank was to lower the radius of operation to 150 miles, from 200, and fit a new engine. The engine picked for this diet was simply described as a 'Junkers engine'. One would immediately see that the complaints against the use of foreign engines still stood, while Martel, now promoted to Assistant Director of Mechanisation, was on hand to point out that the Junkers engine was still extremely immature, and therefore should not be included. Although there would have been some certain irony in a German engine powering a new line of British tanks, just as the Rolls Royce Kestrel engine powered the first of the Luftwaffe's new planes, this idea never came to pass.

The next weight-saving idea was to use cutting-edge technology. At that time, the frames of the tanks were built by riveting steel together, to which the armour was fixed. The suggestion was to use high-tensile steel with the joints welded for the frame. The design department had no idea if this was even possible, or if the technique had been perfected, and thus the Institute of Welding was to be contacted to find out if the suggested method was possible and, if not, if research into this field could be conducted.

Another meeting was held on 26 August to select a parent company for the building of the two prototypes. At first Vulcan Foundry was chosen but that company was producing the A.12 Matilda, a tank requiring a large amount of hand grinding to get the hull to the correct armour thickness. This, in turn, slowed the process of construction. With so much capacity taken up by the A.12, another company was considered. This time LMS Railway of Crewe was selected, maybe not entirely by chance it appears. The locomotive engineer selected to build the A.14 was Mr H. Ivatt, a friend of General Davidson; they had known each other since the First World War. Equally, the discussions on width and railway loading gauge for the A.15 may have influenced the choice of a railway construction company.

In November the mock-up of the A.14 was complete, and three officers from various armour schools were selected to view it with a fighting officer's eye but there is no record of the report that Major Harland and Captains Carmichael and Berkley-Miller filed.

With a war hurtling towards the British, in 1938 the confusing mess of cruiser, heavy cruiser and, potentially, a new class of medium began to make itself felt. Indeed, it seems that an awful lot of effort was expended by the War Office determining what each tank was and explaining the minute differences between tanks. Here the story starts to get mixed up with several other tanks, and indeed spawns new ones.

For nearly a year until December 1938, the A.14 project disappeared from the record. Then things started to move when a limited production of A.14s was scheduled to start in 1939. At the same time, increasing the armour value of the A.14 above 30mm was to be investigated. The branch detailed to review the armour arrangements had already been at work on redesigning the A.14. This proposal was to mount a V8 version of the standard Thornycroft RY12 engine (termed the RY8), transversely across the hull, not lengthways as was normal, which would enable the tank to be shorter. This proposal also included the idea of removing the sub-turrets on the front of the hull; however, they were re-installed on the roof of the main

One of the few pictures of the A.14 to exist. Here it is sitting on a Scammell tank transporter. The turret is rotated to the rear, and the opening for the gun mount is plated over.

turret, complete with the gunners for each sub-turret, creating a five-man turret! One cannot, even now, begin to work out how this arrangement was to work as the machine-gun turret gunners' legs, at the very least, would have been protruding into the fighting compartment. This contraption was given the designation A.19 and it seems from later suggestions that the turret ring would have been the massive size for that time, of 64 inches (5 feet and 4 inches/1.6 metres). It is curious, considering that the A.15 project was ended due to its four-man turret, that the mechanisation board thought they could succeed with a five-man turret, where they had previously failed with a smaller number of crew.

Due to the large number of unknowns involved in the design, and the lack of power plant, it was agreed that the A.19 could not be produced in 1939. However, authorisation was given to continue work on the tank. The main sticking point was that the Thornycroft RY8 did not as yet exist. Indeed it was later stated that the entire A.19 project was dependent on the RY8. In January 1939 a meeting was held at the John Thornycroft works in Reading where the War Office laid out the requirements: the RY8 needed to produce 200hp at 2,000rpm with an emergency back-up of running at 2,400rpm for one hour required. It had to be able to run on grade three fuel.

With several tanks needing this engine, there was some pressure to produce it and, foreseeing a bottleneck in producing crank components, it was urged that an order for two engines be placed immediately. Thornycrofts had submitted a price of £7,000 for two engines but had stressed that this was not a carefully worked out estimate.

Davidson referred to this as 'buying a pig in a poke' and refused to make the purchase until some further reassurances could be obtained. The government and Thornycrofts remained in disagreement until March when a meeting was held and Thornycrofts agreed to lower the sum by £1,000 and take on a consultant, Henry Ricardo, who had previously designed the engine for the Mk V tank of the First World War and had worked on the Merlin engine. The engine also needed to be in production within six months. At the start of February 1939 financial backing for the project was given but it was not until February 1940 that the engine had finished its proof test. On 24 May the project was cancelled, and with it the A.19.

The monstrous A.19 turret lived on, with suggestions to mount the five-man turret on the A.15 Crusader and a modified, lengthened A.13 Mk III, possibly an early version of the Covenanter, all of which came to naught.

The A.14 story did not end with the A.19. In January 1939 the two prototypes being produced by the LMSR came under review and the decision to keep the A.14E1, as designed and produced to the existing schematic as soon as possible, was taken. However, the A.14E2 would have its weight brought down to 24 tons. This decision was driven by the Army getting a new type of pontoon bridge with an upper weight limit of 24 tons, at the time the limit that bridging technology could deliver.

During this time the A.14E1 had been under construction at LMSR's workshops in Kentish Town. Some problems with component supply in the suspension had delayed it, but in November 1938 the tank was nearing completion and it was ready for its trials on 18 May 1939. Although the tank was running, a fault had occurred in the steering, but this was not seen as a major problem and could easily be fixed.

That is as far as the A.14 seems to have progressed. In April 1939 the tank was compared against the A.15 Crusader and was deemed uneconomical due to its weight and the higher number of man hours needed. It was also suggested that the A.14E2 be completed, but with an A.19 turret. However, Davidson was still reluctant to proceed with the A.14, and summoned a meeting of all concerned. This meeting was held on 26 June 1939 and was opened by Davidson announcing that a picture of a new German medium had been obtained. It was one of the *Neubaufahrzeug* tanks, although which of the two designs is not clear. What followed may have been this German tank's only victory over an enemy tank. Due to its size and dimensions it was guessed that the armour on it was only 25mm, which was close to the actual thickness. Due to the appearance of this tank the General Staff now had a requirement for a tank armoured to 40mm basis, weighing under 24 tons and with a speed of 25mph. The meeting recognised this was more than likely unobtainable.

The meeting had two tanks to consider, the A.14E2 modified again to meet the requirement and the modified A13 Mk III. Unable to choose, those attending had the idea of inviting Mr Ivatt along to another meeting and letting him decide the future course for the LMSR. This meeting was held on 30 June 1939, and the cases for both tanks were put forward. Mr Ivatt, and his companion, Mr Caldwell, unsurprisingly selected the A.13 option as the easier tank for LMSR to produce. The partly-completed A.14E2 would be used as spares to keep the A.14E1 running as long as possible, and thus the project faded into history with the A.14E1 being used as an testbed vehicle.

Back in 1937, when Davidson was being convinced to start the A.14 project he also had another tank design that he was not using. This would be designated the A.16 and run in parallel development to the A.14. In many discussions, the two would be compared as they competed against each other. Despite this, they were not competing designs, and it just shows how strange were British thoughts of the period, since the A.16 was sometimes called a 'battlecruiser' class, while the A.14 was a medium. Considering the previously described role of the heavy cruiser, and the existence of the medium tank, it is impossible to say how they differed in the minds of those who assigned classes to these designs.

On 27 November 1937 Davidson was being urged by other departments to proceed with the A.16. The main factor in the start of the A.16 programme was cost. Using standard A.13 components, Nuffield Mechanisation Ltd considered it possible to produce a heavy cruiser at much lower cost than normal. Their opening offer was £15,000 for two pilot models, from scratch. Thus the mock-up was ordered, along with research. However, in December, it was decided that the mock-up would be constructed at the Royal Ordnance factory at Woolwich.

In January 1938 the first scheme for how the A.16 would be engineered appeared from Nuffields. The plan was to take an A.13 final drive and reduce the ratio, thus making the set-up smaller. This allowed for larger brakes to deal with the much heavier weight, due to thicker armour than the A.13. The A.16 had the same armour as the A.14, at 30mm basis. Davidson, however, still lacked enthusiasm and refused to sanction a pilot model due to the A.13E2 still being under development. Another concern of his was the lack of modern tracks; images of the early A.13 prototypes show simple, crude metal plates for tracks.

Another delay came from a batch of missing drawings concerning the A.16 which were chased up with some considerable haste. At the same time, Nuffields were able to report that they had despatched drawings of components to a company called Poldersteel for quotations. One can only imagine how this company had been selected, or if it elicited any comments from the government, since the company was in Austria!

By mid-February a group of design experts (including Martel) was able to offer reassurances that the mistakes in the A.13 design would not be repeated, and pointed out that the price was so low that there should be some movement. Because of these considerations, a single soft-boat prototype was ordered. A considerable portion of the money came from the official cancellation of the A.15 which freed up £10,000.

By 1 March the first drawings of the fighting compartment, and a new design of shock absorbers, were ready, and the government had arranged for armour plate to be provided from Hadfields. A day later, Martel met Hotblack again, as the latter was now serving in another part of the War

THE TANKS WITHOUT A WAR

The only two photographs known to exist of the A.13E1, these were taken from a trials report on the A.13E1. The trials report detailed the numerous mechanical faults the tank suffered. Luckily these pictures serve to show how basic were the tracks of early British cruisers.

Office. Both were accompanied by several other officers, including the commander of 1 Tank Brigade. Together they inspected the mock-up of the A.16 at the Royal Ordnance factory in Woolwich. Most of the design was authorised, with special praise seemingly aimed at the mounting of the smoke mortar. This piece was an ECLA breech-loader, located in an extension of the front turret plate. For some time the ability to fire smoke had been desired. For example, in 1936 an officer of the tank unit deployed to help quell the Arab revolt in Palestine had suggested that a smoke mortar would have been extremely useful; originally he suggested something along the lines of a Stokes mortar.

One fault that was spotted by the viewing officers, was that the sub-turret gunners had insufficient legroom, and so the turrets would have to be redesigned. Nuffields had been carrying out a large amount of research on new tracks for the A.16 which culminated in June when a Mr Clarke, presumably an engineer of the company, handed over the finalised designs. Nuffields then requested that production of the tracks begin immediately.

At the end of June Martel reported back to the Mechanisation Board on the particulars of the engine and transmission of the A.16. On the last point, there was consideration of adopting a single type of Wilson gearbox for both A.13 and A.16. As an alternative, Martel had visited the Cotal works in France where he had viewed their electrically-controlled double gearbox, which was suitable for the A.16. One of course remembers the decision not to accept foreign engines for supply reasons and wonders if this also applied to the gearbox. Either way, the board made another choice: LMSR would get the contract to produce the A.16 turret, as it was similar to the A.14 turret. A few days later another meeting was held at which the date of completion for the pilot model was announced as 'the end of 1938'. However, despite this, due to other commitments, Nuffields could not start production until 1940. Initial production tanks would have the Liberty engine, but the Meadows 500hp engine or a CI diesel engine should be considered for future builds, as would the Wilson gearbox, which was discounted for the first production run as too immature in its development.

The completion date for the A.16E1 was further refined on 1 July to 'the beginning of October'. Nuffields stated that they would make every endeavour to reach this date, even going so far as to manufacture components they had already sub-contracted out. Two weeks later another pilot model of the A.16 was ordered.

The A.16E2 was, the Mechanisation Board very forcefully warned, not to be used as 'an excuse to launch out into a number of alternative designs'.

THE TANKS WITHOUT A WAR

This, and the next image, are pictures of the A.16E1. One would presume that the ECLA smoke mortar would be fitted into the opening on the top right of the turret front.

The very next action, on the face of it, seems to fly directly in the face of this warning. Davidson visited the Vickers Armstrong works at Chertsey in mid-February 1939 to inspect the A.18, which we will look at later. Upon seeing the arrangement of the hull machine guns on the A.18, he desired that the A.16E2 be modified to match. This would have required a re-work of the driver's compartment. As this would have unforeseen implications on the tank all further work was halted, and the tank was never completed.

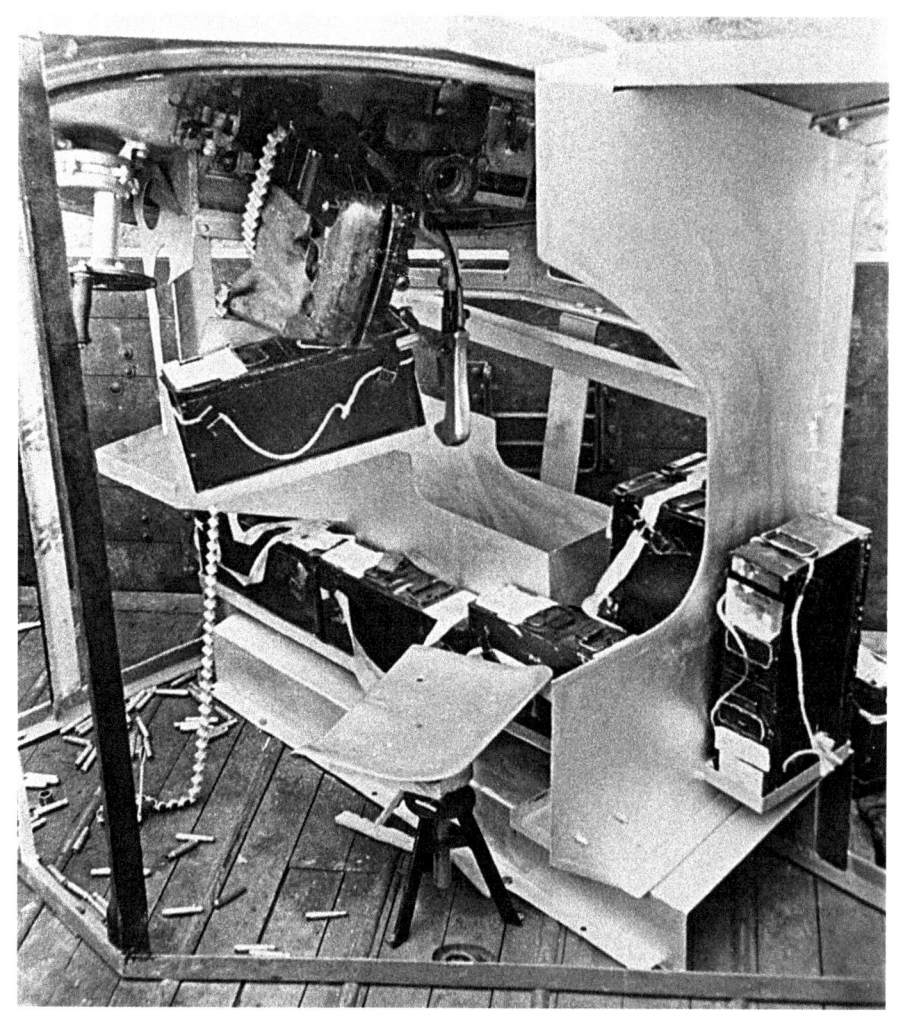

A shot of the internals of the A.18 sub turret. An example of the sub-turret was actually built and mounted on the bed of a truck for testing, which is why the floor and sides of this picture are made of wooden planks.

THE TANKS WITHOUT A WAR

Side aspect of the almost completed A.16E1.

The complete A.16E1 was delivered on 19 September 1939. It was not in running condition, due to a failure of the final drive. Instead of returning the tank, it was accepted simply because it was not going to go into production, so there seemed to be very little point in sending it back for a fix. It may be that the declaration of war had caused a focusing of minds and the culling of quite a few programmes. As to the fate of the A.16E1, it seems that it went the way of most failed prototypes, to be used in Frankenstein-like experiments by the Army. In February 1940, when the Thornycroft RY8 finished its proof test, it was listed as ready to be fitted to the A.16E1, when that vehicle was made available. A worse fate awaited it after they finished with it. The utterly smashed hulk of the A.16E1 was last seen in 1985 at Hangmoor Hill ranges. After forty years as a target hulk it was not considered worthwhile to recover and restore.

There is one final entry on the A.16 story: in 1941 a final bill for the A.16E1 and incomplete A.16E2. It came to £15,600. 2s. 1d.

Effectively the A.14 and A.16 seemed to be fighting for the same spot in the army as a 'battlecruiser' or 'medium' class of tank. Earlier, the A.14 was only ever seen as a test vehicle, yet there seems to have been discussion of producing it as a combat vehicle. On 16 December 1938 both vehicles came under scrutiny: the choice was between it (more expemsive but better at ditch crossing and ready sooner) and the cheaper A.16, which was within the General Staff weight requirements, and was a smaller tank. The

FORGOTTEN TANKS AND GUNS OF THE 1920s, 1930s AND 1940s

The last known pictures of the A.16E1, taken on the ranges at Hangmoor. What happened next is impossible to say, but it is likely that it was hauled off by a scrap merchant.

problems with the A.16 were that it would be in production much later and the Christie suspension, although proven, had given trouble when loaded up to the A.16's weight. In the end the A.16 became the preferred option. In any case, due to events, neither saw life past a single prototype and a half-complete second prototype.

Previously in this narrative I have mentioned the A.18, briefly, and how it affected the development, and demise, of the A.16E2. On 18 June 1938, Hotblack wrote to Martel, and a couple of other officers, outlining that Vickers had spare facilities and were pushing for design work. The two options for work were either a heavy cruiser, for which the A.16 already filled the slot, or an 'improved light cruiser'. What followed was some interesting discussion between the departments regarding anti-tank weapons. First the departments looked at current hand-held and small-arms performance, and tried to project where they would be in a few years. Oddly for small-arms performance, a .276 (about 6.9mm) calibre bullet was used, and it was stated that this would likely be the standard bullet in five years' time. The British did start looking at that calibre, but not until the early 1950s. Also under consideration were 20mm anti-tank weapons. It was quickly stated that a tank for protection against these weapons would need to be in the 40mm range now, and rapidly increased to 50mm which, to British minds, was entering the Infantry-tank class.

In the case of larger anti-tank guns, one of the departments did admit that a 25-pounder had been tested as an anti-tank gun, and that it had penetrated 70mm at 825 yards range. Reassuringly, the writer said that it was unlikely that anti-tank guns would reach this calibre in five years, although guns around 55mm were possible, as the Germans were looking at a 52mm, and the British had just started work on such a gun, which would eventually be the 6-pounder. With it impossible to armour against contemporary threats it was decided only to protect against hand-held weapons such as anti-tank rifles and smaller.

From what can be seen, there was no difference between this improved light cruiser and a heavy cruiser which neatly shows the mess of definitions that plagued British tank development of the time.

At a meeting to discuss the situation in July, the War Office said it had requirements for an infantry tank in the 70mm class, and two tanks in the 30mm class, one armed with nothing but Czech ZB machine guns, the other with a 2-pounder and the usual array of five air-cooled ZB machine guns.

The Vickers representatives admitted that they had been thinking along the lines of the 30mm class armed with a 2-pounder and so detailed

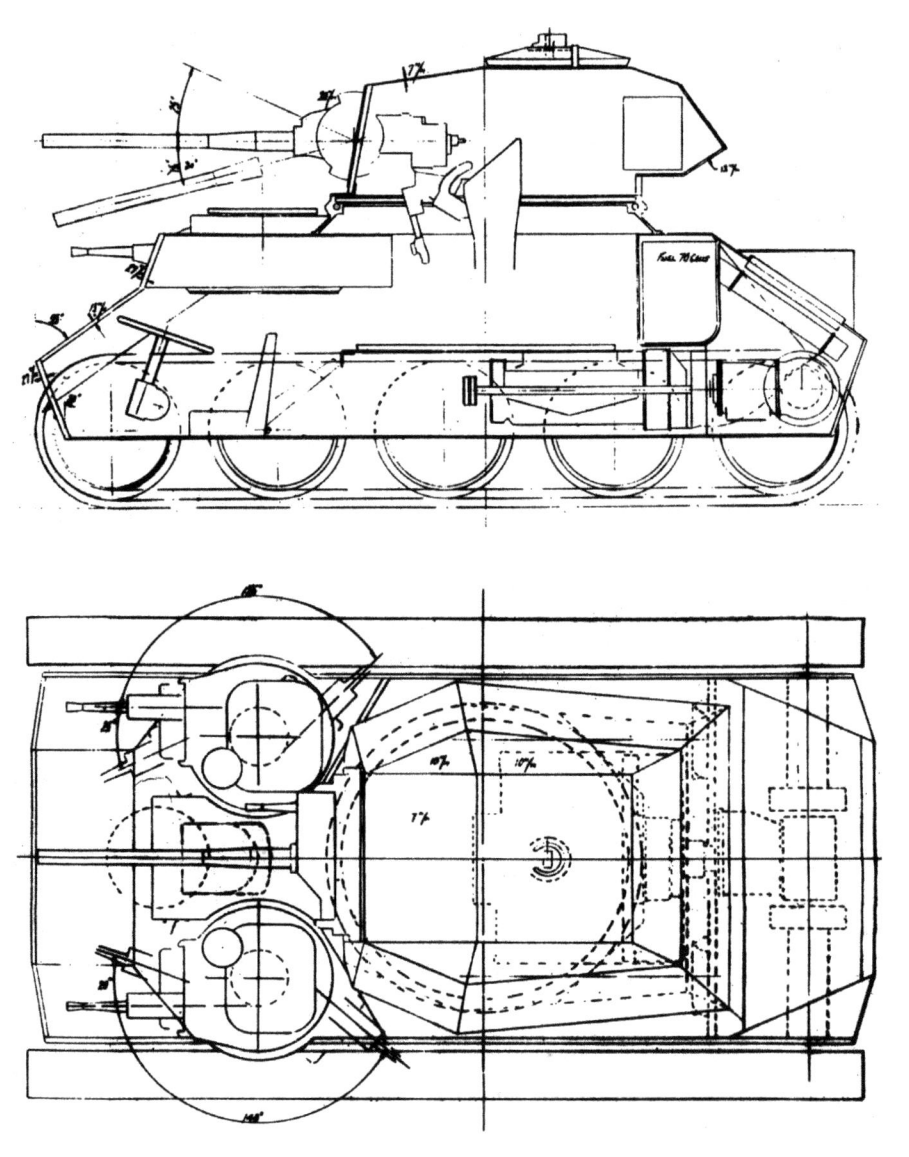

The plans for the first version of the A.18 which show the incredibly top-heavy, short appearance, and the location of the engine. One dreads to think how unstable this tank would have been cross-country due to its short track run.

discussions started. One thing that Vickers were keen to stress was their new flexible track steering, as fitted to the A.17. They made a number of claims about this new track. One was that with it rolling resistance was one quarter less than the conventional track on the Mk VIB light tank, and that there was much less power lost. Because of this latter claim, a much higher power-to-weight ratio, and a smaller engine, could be implemented than would be usual. Several department heads questioned this claim on several occasions, but Vickers were adamant that they could get the weight down to twelve tons and reach 30mph in a 30mm armoured machine, with a Meadows 160hp engine.

One other stumbling block was the range. The requirements were for a tank with 200 miles range a figure that could only be achieved with external drop tanks. At first the board wanted them armoured, but this would have driven the weight up. So self-sealing jettisonable fuel tanks were accepted. The other curiosity was that the Meadows was a flat-type engine mounted under the turret, meaning that the tank was much shorter on the rear than would be expected, but much taller, with the look of a tank that had been cut in half. One flaw of having such a short track run was that the trench crossing was only 6 feet, later increased to 6 feet 6 inches. Another complaint that Vickers had to address from their initial design was the gun depression. Vickers had designed for -15 degrees, but the minimum was to be increased to -20. A soft-boat and mock-up was ordered, to be ready within eighteen months and a second pilot model ready six months after that.

The new and improved A.18 sub-turret, fitted to the truck bed for testing.

The mock-up was ready by October that year. However, later, in February 1939, some new design changes had been made. These were the ones that had a knock-on effect on the A.16E2. Instead of using normal sub-turrets, these had been replaced by a pair of sloping plates on either side of the driver, with the twin machine guns mounted in them. The guns had a traverse of 115 degrees, with elevation of +15/-10 degrees. The mounting saved about 7 hundredweight (just over a third of a ton) from the overall weight. This was a revolutionary step as, previously, the myriad of sub-turrets had taken a considerable part of the overall weight of the tank. There was concern about the level of protection these mounts provided and a mock-up for firing tests was requested and even ordered. When this mock-up was about 60 per cent complete, on 21 October 1939, the A.18 project was cancelled and all contracts closed.

Postscript

Even as I wrote the last words in the previous chapter, I was reminded that new discoveries in the field of British armour are still being made. The day after I completed the last paragraph on the A.18, a friend sent me an image in which may be seen lines of tanks with, sitting in the rearmost line, the unmistakable bulk of the Modified Monster, the A.14. What makes this even weirder is that the caption, which may be wrong, claimed it was taken at Aberdeen Proving ground in the USA. Did the A.14 play some part in the development of US armour as well? Is there a further story to tell?

The picture that is marked 'Aberdeen'. The A.14E1 sits in the second row next to the Churchill gun carrier, still covered by tarpaulins over the engine deck. It is pictured with the same tarpaulins in the only other known picture.

Either way the picture is post-war, as the presence of a German Bergpanther proves; so the Modified Monster lived for quite some time.

That is what I love about this field: so little has been done in researching British technology in general and armour in particular that there are so many new discoveries waiting to appear.

Sources

Lurking in the Jungle:
UK National Archives, Kew, Surrey; Japanese National Archives; and Seon Eun Ae.

Battle Wing:
UK National Archives.

From the Sea, through the Blood to the Green fields Beyond:
UK National Archives; Tank Museum, Bovington; and Churchill College Archives.

You Disston my tank:
Ipswich Records Office; www.tanks-encyclopedia.com; and Andrew Hills.

The Smoking Gun:
UK National Archives

Hail Hydran:
Andrew Hills; UK National Archives; and David Fletcher, *Universal Carrier 1936-48* (Osprey, Botley.)

The Cambridge Camal:
UK National Archives

Schwimmpanzer 36:
UK National Archives

Recoil Control:
UK National Archives; Defence Capability Centre (Shrivenham).

FORGOTTEN TANKS AND GUNS OF THE 1920s, 1930s AND 1940s

The Soldierless tank:
UK National Archives

The Secret Life of the Infantry Tank:
Imperial War Museum; and Tank Museum, Bovington.

The Tanks without a war:
UK National Archives; and Tank Museum, Bovington